D E N I M

DENIM

AN AMERICAN LEGEND

TEXT BY IAIN FINLAYSON

A Fireside Book
Published by Simon & Schuster Inc.
New York London Toronto Sydney Tokyo Singapore

The publishers would like to thank the photographers and agencies listed below for the use of their material in this book.

Title page Guess? Inc/Photograph by Wayne Maser. **6** Western Americana. **8** *top and middle* Western Americana, *bottom* Popperfoto. **10** Library of Congress/Photograph by Walker Evans. **13** *top* Western Americana, *bottom* Hulton-Deutsch Collection. **14** *top left* and *right* Magnum/Photograph by Henri Cartier-Bresson, *bottom* Magnum/ Photograph by Paul Fusco. **16** *top left* Popperfoto, *top right* and *bottom* Bettman Archive. **17** Bettman Archive. **19** Wrangler. **20** Rex Features. **23** *top* Magnum/Photograph by Henri Cartier-Bresson, *bottom* Magnum/ Photograph by Chris Steele-Perkins. **24** Magnum/Photograph by Henri Cartier-Bresson. **26** *top* Hulton-Deutsch Collection, *bottom* Magnum/ Photograph by Henri Cartier-Bresson. **28** *left* Gamma, *right* Rex Features. **31** Andy Warhol, 1971 Rolling Stones album cover. **32** McCann Erickson. **35** Gamma. **36** Rex Features. **39** Magnum/ Photograph by Chris Steele-Perkins. **40** *top left* Camera Press/ Photograph by Jan Kopec, *top right* Photograph by Monica Curtin, *bottom* Camera Press/Photograph by Homer Sykes.

43 Photograph by Spencer Rowell. **44** Photograph by Anthony Crickmay. **47** Wrangler. **49** Hulton-Deutsch Collection. **50** Magnum/ Photograph by Sebastio Salgado. **51** *top* Magnum/Photograph by Robert Capa, *bottom left* Monica Kinley/Photograph by Ida Kar, *bottom right* Camera Press/Photograph by Richard Open. **53** *left* Hulton-Deutsch Collection, *right* Camera Press. **54** *left* Hulton-Deutsch Collection, *right* Hulton-Deutsch Collection. **57** Photograph by Kenneth Griffiths. **58** *top left* Camera Press, *top right* Popperfoto, *bottom left* Magnum/Photograph by Eve Arnold, *bottom right* Camera Press/Photograph by Tony Drabble. **60** Hulton-Deutsch Collection.

63 Valentino. **64** Perry Ellis/1987 advertisement. **66** Photograph by Monica Curtin. **69 & 70** Bartle, Bogle, Hegarty. **72** Photographs by Monica Curtin. **75** Camera Press. **77** Calvin Klein/Photograph by Richard Avedon. **78** Magnum/Photograph by Dennis Stock. **79** *top left, bottom left* and *right* Rex Features, *top right* Photograph by Astrid Kircherr. **80** Guess? Inc. **83 & 85** Calvin Klein/Photographs by Bruce Weber. **86** Photograph by Monica Curtin. **88** Photograph by Kenneth Griffiths. **90** Photograph by Spencer Rowell. **93 & 94** Photograph by Kenneth Griffiths. **96** Magnum/Photograph by Henri Cartier-Bresson. **99** Premier Photographic/Photograph by Mark Liddell. **100** Magnum/ Photograph by Erich Hartmann. **101** Bettman Archive. **103** Popperfoto. **104** Magnum/Photograph by Chris Steele-Perkins. **107** Flashbacks. **109** Magnum/Photograph by Eli Reed. **111** Photograph by Spencer Rowell. **112** Photograph by Anthony Crickmay. **114** Magnum/ Photograph by Thomas Hopker. **116** Photograph by Spencer Rowell. **119** Rex Features. **120** Photograph by Anthony Crickmay. **122** Calvin Klein. **124** Valentino. **127** Photograph by Anthony Crickmay. **128** Photograph by Monica Curtin.

Fireside

Simon & Schuster Building

Rockefeller Center

1230 Avenue of the Americas

New York, New York 10020

Designed and produced by Parke Sutton Limited,
Magdalen House, 1 Bull Close Road,
Norwich NR3 1NG, England

Printed and bound in Hong Kong for Imago

1 3 5 7 9 10 8 6 4 2

Library of Congress Cataloging in Publication Data
Finlayson, Iain.
Denim: an American legend : text / by
Iain Finlayson.
p. cm.
"A Fireside book."
ISBN 0-671-72368-5
1. Jeans (Clothing)—History. 2. Jeans
(Clothing)—Advertising.
3. Levi Strauss and Company—History.
4. Denim—History.
5. Fashion—United States—History—20th century.
I. Title.
GT2085.F56 1990
338.4'7687113—dc20 90-33178
CIP

CONTENTS

Old-timer' Forty-niner panning for gold, busting his butt in original denim jeans.

FROM THE KLONDYKE TO KLEIN

IN 1850 A YOUNG BAVARIAN IMMIGRANT named Levi Strauss arrived in Eldorado. The fabled land of gold was, in the event, further north than the Spanish conquistadores, who had overthrown South American civilizations in their lustful search for legendary treasure, had suspected. In fact, Eldorado was discovered by accident on January 24, 1848, when James Wilson Marshall, an emigrant Scottish carpenter, picked out some glittering nuggets of gold, about the size of peas, from the mill race at Sutter's sawmill which still exists at Coloma, some fifty miles east of Sacramento. The prospect of fabulous wealth was confirmed by the government in Washington in December '48, and the Gold Rush of '49 was on. Levi Strauss was a year behind the gold-fevered 'Forty Niners' who battered their way across a continent to California; but he was a year ahead of John L.B. Soule, an Indiana newspaperman who, in an editorial in the Terre Haute Express in 1851, advised those who had not already lit out to "Go West, young man, go West!"

Levi Strauss was twenty years old, and had come to sell canvas for tents and wagon covers to the hundred thousand or more prospectors who had invaded California. They had arrived with not much more than the clothes they stood up in, and whatever minimal equipment they hadn't lost or abandoned on the long trek West. They had started, most of them, from St. Joseph, Missouri, following the Platte River across Nebraska to the Rockies where their real problems began. The survivors were tough: they had burned in deserts and frozen in mountain passes; endured starvation and drought; been attacked by Indians and poisoned by mosquitoes; lost or abandoned wives, families, livestock and wagons; gone mad and murdered one another; been decimated by cholera and dried out by dysentery. By the time they reached

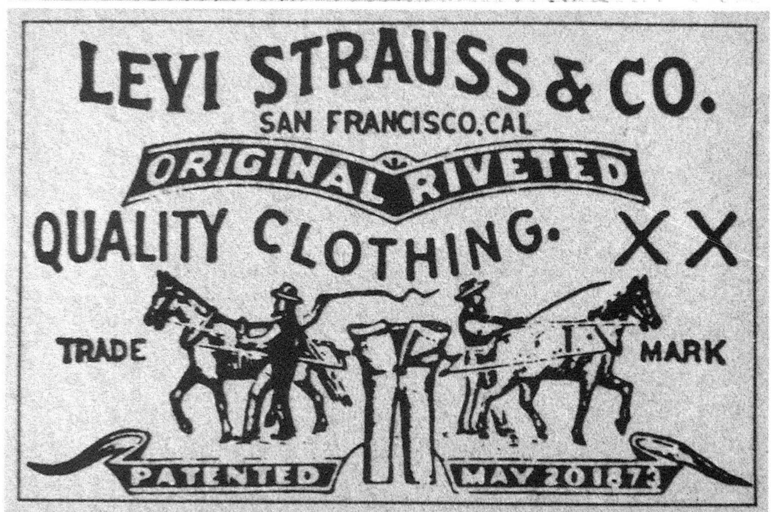

DAWN OF DENIM

Staff members of the Levi Strauss clothing factory, San Francisco, nineteenth century.

Levi Strauss blue denims brand label commemorating a publicity stunt.

Warehouse workers baling cotton, wearing unriveted denim – the back pockets have burst at the seams.

the American River they had been stripped of everything but the driving will to hit the motherlode that ran from north of Sutter's mill to Mariposa, one hundred and twenty miles of shining gold.

The richest diggings had smartly been appropriated by Californian ranchers – the 'Nobs', the founding families of California, who created San Francisco from a shanty town of tents and shacks and built their fantastical mansions on Nob Hill. But the swarming prospectors settled to scratch and pan for what was left of the treasure. Hunkering down in the mud and dirt was rough work. Pants gave out at the knees and the butt, seams split under constant stress, but the gold-diggers would go bare-ass naked if necessary before the gold light died in their eyes. They didn't need tents (they'd sleep rough – they'd slept rougher) and they didn't need wagon covers (what was there left to cover?). They needed pants – which Levi Strauss, after consulting with a San Francisco tailor, was ready to supply. The boilermaker pattern they evolved was a 'waist-high overall', and the first pairs of Levi's were made of brown tenting canvas. Strauss sold dozens; then he sold hundreds. Then he opened a shop in San Francisco.

Tent canvas was tough, but a durable cotton fabric known as *serge de Nîmes*, manufactured and worn in the South of France, was tougher. He imported it by the boatload, in trading ships manned mostly by Genoese sailors. From *serge de Nîmes* came the word 'denim'. From Genoese came the word 'jeans'. Levi's denim jeans were dyed with indigo, a pure, deep blue dye manufactured from the leaves of *Indigofera*, a tropical plant that had once, before the Revolution, been grown, harvested, and processed on the slave plantations of South Carolina. By the 1850s, it was mostly imported from India, though within forty years indigo was

Sharecropper in denim dungarees, the utility workwear of the West. Photograph by Walker Evans.

synthetically reproduced in the laboratory in 1897 by a German chemist, Adolf von Baeyer.

The design of Levi's jeans was nothing to write home to the fashion papers about: they were built to be moved around in, for body protection, and durability. Prospectors stuffed their pockets with mineral samples, fraying and bursting the seams at stress points. In 1873 a Nevada tailor suggested to Levi Strauss that rustproof copper rivets must solve the problem. Strauss even placed a rivet, if company legend is true, at the base of the fly – until "a customer stood too close to a camp fire and suffered from an overheated rivet". In the same year, Levi Strauss himself introduced the trademark stitched double arc design on the back pockets to suggest the shape of an American eagle's wings. The stitching was purely decorative – it served no useful purpose – but it was perhaps a tribute to the spirit of American enterprise and opportunism, dogged optimism, and capacity for survival that had infected and stimulated Strauss during the first roaring days in the California gold fields. In 1886 he added a leather patch to the waistband of his jeans to commemorate an inspired advertising stunt that involved two horses, pulling in opposite directions, trying to pull apart a pair of Levi's. The horses lost.

Those prospectors who had been bilked of their claims or sold out, who had either scraped together a nest-egg or given up in disgust, moved back East or settled to more reliable work as farmers, ranchers, cowboys, lumberjacks, railroadmen, or storekeepers. They still needed pants, and Levi's were still popular as workwear. Demand for denim in California was enormous and constant, but had nothing to do with fashion or high style. Denim was the staple workwear of the West, rarely crossing the Rockies until the 1930s when rich Easterners on vacation, stimulated by books and movies about the legendary exploits of cowboys and Indians and the days of the Gold Rush, trekked Westward as tourists. The journey was still something of a minor adventure, and the customs of the West – not to say Hollywood – were strange and fantastical to most sober Easterners. They still are: California appears to have a near-monopoly on weird. They ate cowboy chow, rode cowboy-style, twirled lariats, wore Stetson hats, and bought cowboy clothes. Levi's travelled back, east of Mississippi, dark blue and stiff with heroic tradition.

Denim's transition from West to East had very little to do with any empathies the well-to-do might feel for California roughnecks: it had a certain cachet only when associated with the work of Claire McCardell, who is now regarded as the first and finest American ready-to-wear designer of the century. Born in 1905 in Maryland, she produced her first collection as designer for Townley Frocks in 1938. In that year, she showed the first of her classics – a waistless, dartless, bias-cut tent dress that was known as 'The Monastic'. Her full genius emerged in the 1940s in New York: designing for the style of life and attitudes of free-moving American women, Claire McCardell became a byword for clean, functional, casual, comfortable, relaxed and sporty clothes that, though easy to wear and simple in concept, were also glamorous and fashionable. She created classics such as 'The Popover', an unstructured and waistless dress that wrapped around the body; the 'Empire' line that looked inevitably modern; body stockings based on the concept of the leotard; and 'The Shirtwaister' dress that remains popular to this day. Her clothes were eminently copiable, and her preferred fabrics were cheap and easy to obtain – jersey, ticking, cotton calico and denim.

Levi Strauss advertisement, about 1910; creation of mythic image. Gold-rich prospectors didn't just need denim – they needed brokers and lawyers.

Cartier-Bresson photographs denim, cloth cap and top hat style. Taking five, putting his back to the wheel, easy in the shade.

Her inspirations came largely from functional clothes that had been worn for centuries or generations by working people and children. She would not have been surprised by the 1960s' fashion for 'ethnic chic' which derived from peasant and workers' costume. Naturally, in the 1940s, she looked at the miners and the ranch hands of California and the middle-west, recognizing the durability and design potential of denim which she used to create fashions for urban women whose lives were fast, active, and tough on clothes. More than any one designer, Claire McCardell helped to introduce denim to the urban environment, to fashion it into clothes for working women whose lives were efficient and energetic. Denim wore well and still looked good after washing, cleaning, or at the end of a hard day. Denim, for the first time, achieved urban chic and an all-important cachet among the fashionable cognoscenti of the East Coast.

Denim and jeans, for all their French origin and Italian name, are strictly American in style and tradition. Denim was utilitarian, with no status signals, until the 1950s. Denim was as plain and unaffected as dirt under the bed. If young American girls had worn jeans with sloppy sweaters for chores, school, bicycling, or loafing around, they were classed as 'tomboys' aping their brothers. But even the most hard-nosed Junior Miss would break out the chiffon for a date with a boyfriend or the Junior Prom. Natalie Wood never stomped the West Side in jeans. Rita Moreno – in feistier moments – might have thought about it, maybe. Jeans were for punk kids, macho adolescent males – the Jets. In pre-war and pre-Rock and Roll America, denim had expressed only a basic concept of poverty and hard manual labor, overlaid with the masculine, free-ranging image of the cowboy who lived more or less outside the conventions

DUSTBOWL DENIM

No money, no status, no hope beyond basic survival. Denim is still redolent of the mythic hardships of the Great Depression, of tenacity in adversity, of the human spirit that endures even in despair. There is stony stoicism in the face of the sharecropper, bleak humour in the black face, united loyalty in the nuclear family, and persistence in the eyes of a young couple. Denim perfectly symbolized the dirt-poor, dogged determination of the individual in adversity.

and strictly-enforced rules of urban society. Jeans became associated with an element of non-conformity that appealed to the developing youth culture. In post-war Europe, in the 1950s, blue jeans became a status symbol associated with the new music that, in the beginning, was evolving from Country and Western.

Jeans and Rock and Roll were American, and were appropriated by 1950s kids as symbols and vehicles of liberation from the stale, sedate culture of their parents. Denim was the natural fabric for a new, classless, transatlantic culture based on youth and aggression. Alison Lurie, in *The Language of Clothes*, remarks: "Like the savage who slings a bearskin around his shoulders, or sticks eagle's feathers in his hair, the contemporary European teenager in his Levi's is practicing contagious magic: he subconsciously believes that the power and virtue of America is contained in those jeans and will rub off on him." She also points out that "at any given period some countries are chic and others dowdy. What makes a country fashionable in most cases is economic and political alliance or political power. . . . At the deepest level, this phenomenon is the expression of magical thinking." America's entry into World War II, its post-war Marshall Plan, its powerful role in Nato, its Imperialist expansion, its influential movies and music, its overt aggression manifested in speech and behavior, its glamour and glitter, all combined to establish America and its culture as dominant and attractive to the young. Europe, in post-war conditions, was certainly dowdy.

Imports of genuine American jeans, particularly Levi's, confirmed the status of those lucky or sharp enough to get them. The point was to look, act and feel American. Cheap copies of American jeans flooded the European market, but the kids were not fooled – their eagle eye

WRANGLERS

Wranglers Jeans: hog-tied at the hoe-down – a little light bondage in the 1940s; The clone family sticks together in the 1950s; Hold this one by your other ear, honey – stereo! Disco denim in the 1960s.

The King – Elvis – in dirt road denim.

for status detail didn't overlook shoddy fabric and workmanship. The fakes didn't fit either the body or the image. American jeans were new, they were sharp, they were neat, they were redolent of a new world; they were beyond fashion – they were essential. They were, like Rock and Roll, profoundly subversive. Jeans were modern – none of the tradition of the American working class was imported with them: blue jeans were for heroes and rebels. Elvis Presley was the rebel hero image personified. Presley wore blue jeans with cowboy boots or crêpe-soled shoes, and Western shirts. He slicked his hair and swung his hips. He opened his mouth and women fainted or were carried away orgasmically screaming. Presley – the Pelvis – was sexual. Elvis was a stud. He curled his lip and millions ecstatically curled their toes. He was Rock and Roll in the hunky flesh, and Rock and Roll represented the power of youth.

Denim, identified with hot-lips and hot-hips Presley, was perfect: any significant youth movement requires either new clothes or that an existing style of dress be invested with new meaning. Presley, and other singers, invested denim with sex and subversion. No dutiful, responsible, conventional adult would dream of wearing denim which was now regarded as an implicit criticism of social conformity and the norms of good citizenship. Jeans, worn casually for leisure and pleasure, subverted the work ethic they were originally created to serve. They were damned from the pulpit, in the press, and by the moral majority. The new movies – *On The Waterfront, East of Eden, Rebel Without A Cause* – reinforced the look. Brando, Dean, and any smoldering, scowling, disaffected hunk in T-shirt, leather jacket, boots, and a pair of denim jeans increased demand. Denim, already iconoclastic, became iconic. Denim, dissociated from its origins, acquired values and vices that were anathema to anyone who did not understand the complex signal system, the life-mode, the social and sexual significances that denim represented. Blue jeans, to anyone who found teenagers resistible and incomprehensible, were symbols of violent immaturity and deliberate challenge to convention.

By the early 1960s jeans were well established as casual wear among teens and early twenties. Fashion styled them suggestively lower on the hips and tighter on the legs. They didn't leave much to the imagination, and Jim ("I wanted to see what it would look like in the spotlight") Morrison of the Doors unzipped his jeans and took out what his fans had been dying to size up. Jeans were guaranteed to shrink and fade with wash and wear. Bought a size larger than necessary, they were bathed, bleached, battered, and roughed up to the required condition of decadence. When they were adequately de-sanitized and de-Sanforized, they were worn flesh-squeezingly tight. First you had to take your shoes off, point your toes like a dancer, and pull the jeans like a panty-hose up the legs and over the ass. Second, you had to lie flat on the floor, breathe in hard, and take tight hold of the zipper with one hand while holding the waistband up with the other. Wriggling while tugging at the crotch was optional, but usually you had to lift your butt from the floor, and the whole thing looked like some advanced technique from the Kama Sutra that had to be practiced alone to get it right. For a smoother fit, and a better basket, you didn't bother with underpants which, in any case, showed naff bumps under the material, so there was an art to not catching, agonizingly, pubic hair as you whopped up the zipper in one fast, straight movement. The effect of rough denim on tender adolescent sexual organs was occasionally – embarrassing. But the eroticizing effect of denim on the naked body was – nice.

Digging it in denim at the hop – let the good times roll.

Meditating the revolution in blue jeans, mediated by Cartier-Bresson.

In *Cities On A Hill*, Frances FitzGerald described how denim hit the hippy trail: "sometime in the mid-Sixties large numbers of white, middle-class young people suddenly and quite spontaneously took off their middle-class clothes and put on the dress of working men – blue jeans – and took up the erotic music of the black working class. The men grew their hair long and the women took to wearing pants (blue jeans, perhaps, with denim jackets). And together they turned on their elders and went on the road. . . . They went looking for their peers, and whether they found them at antiwar demonstrations, at Woodstock, or in India along the ashram routes, the discovery was the same: they were a brother- and sisterhood, and they shared a secret understanding – one not vouchsafed to Eleanor Rigby, or Mr. Jones. The secret was that they alone were real and authentic." First the rockers, now the hippies, identified themselves to one another through their clothes – blue jeans and denim shirts.

So long as the hippy generation believed itself to be a community of equals – brothers and sisters united in idealism – all aspiring to love, peace, social justice, freedom from bourgeois institutions and values – its mode of dress conformed to and reinforced the ideal of equality by being, so far as possible, uniform. Denim was a badge of social ethics, of social community and group identity, that scorned the conventional etiquette of dress. "The counterculture", remarked Frances FitzGerald, "was not an alternate culture so much as an anticulture where all structures and conventions were dissolved. For the young, it was quite precisely a melting pot. It was a melting pot in the original sense where 'all the races of Europe were melting and reforming'. But it was also a melting pot for the remnants of Victorian bourgeois culture that had survived into the Sixties. It was not – as many at the time supposed – an end in itself;

CLASSLESS DENIM

On the streets and in the communes, denim was de rigeur: the classless anti-fashion of the protest movement and high thinking.

rather, it was a beginning. It was the creative ooze from which new life-forms would emerge."

In the late 1960s, European and American students erected and manned the barricades of actual, bloody revolution to protest right-wing attitudes, the nuclear threat, and the Vietnam war. Denim, infinitely adaptable, began to be worn by all classes and conditions to fight – whether physically or otherwise – the battles for peace, social equality, and civil rights. Artists, students, the liberal middle and upper classes, high school kids, even children, adopted denim. Denim and blue jeans, as significators of socialism and liberalism, were – up to a point – anti-fashion. The protestors who rejected the intolerances and injustices of society also rejected its dogmatic fashions set by high-caste fashion designers in the major European and American cities. Denim was street-fashion; denim was – as the hippies had recognized – 'real-life' and 'authentic'. It was, so far as possible, classless and anonymous, consciously and deliberately symbolic of revolution that did not require clothes to symbolize position in a social hierarchy.

In 1969, denim as a badge of street credibility had not seized the rare heights of America's intelligentsia. According to Tom Wolfe, in *Radical Chic and Mau-Mauing the Flak Catchers*, Andrew Stein's party in Southampton on June 29 1969 for Chavez and the grape workers was an affair of unconscious ironies: "The grape workers were all in work clothes, Levi's, chinos, Sears balloon-seat twills, K-Mart sports shirts, and so forth. The socialites, meanwhile, arrived at the height of the 1969 season of bell-bottom silk pants suits, Pucci clings, Dunhill blazers, and Turnbull and Asser neckerchiefs." While out in California, students – not quite regardless of status – were "dressed Revolutionary Street Fighter. After the strike at State, middle-class students didn't show up on campus any more in letter sweaters or those back-to-school items

Dedicated followers of anti-fashion: Madonna and Mick Jagger.

like you see in the McGregor ads. They dressed righteous and 'with the people'. They would have on guerrilla gear that was so righteous that Che Guevara would have had to turn in his beret and get bucked down to company chaplain if he'd come up against it. They would have on berets and hair down to the shoulders, 1958 Sierra Maestra style, and raggedy field jackets and combat boots and jeans, but not Levi's or Slim Jims or Farahs or Wranglers or any of those tailored hip-hugging jeans, but jeans of the people, the black Can't Bust 'Em brand, hod carrier jeans that have an emblem on the back of a hairy gorilla, real *funky* jeans and woolly green socks, the kind that you get at the Army surplus at two pair for twenty-nine cents."

Which was nice and funky and real and credible for white middle-class kids fighting the class war, but the folks they were empathizing with had other aspirations. Tom Wolfe noticed that "the oppressed, the hard-core youth in the ghetto – they aren't into the Can't Bust 'Ems with the gorilla and the Army surplus socks. They're into the James Brown look. They're into the ruffled shirts, the black belted leather pieces from Boyd's on Market Street, the bellcuff herringbones, all that stuff, looking sharp. If you tried to put one of those lumpy lumberjack shirts on them, they'd vomit." Status, even in uniform, will out, and denim was subtly differentiated even among the supposedly classless young. Denim became a blank canvas to be painted, embroidered, studded, patched, fringed, as the Radical Sixties gave itself up to the glamorous Seventies. Rock stars had begun to apply glitter and fashion styling to the basic hippy denim as authentically worn by Haight-Ashbury hippies or as real-life combat gear in the burning streets of Paris. People had got used to wearing denim, and had started playing around with it to the point where cut was vital, the width of flares a matter of critical judgement, and the label all-important: Levi's, Wranglers, Lees, and others spoke a language of their own to different groups. As the hippy/revolutionary youth culture became acceptable – even chic, among trendsetters (among the duplexes and condos of the fashionable rich, as distinct from Haight-Ashbury radicals who were avant-garde rather than chic) it became necessary to integrate the outward symbols of the alternative culture into mainstream society. Clothes were the readiest-available means of expressing sympathy with the look of the anti-culture without actually having to live the life. Clothes implied attitudes and a lifestyle that did not have to be too closely observed in reality. Clothes could give the illusion that a person had 'dropped-out' a little bit – 'real-life' denim became 'lifestyle' denim. In 1971, to confirm social and Seventh Avenue acceptance of denim as safe to wear beyond the barricades, the Coty Fashion Critics Award for world fashion influence – the Seventh Avenue Oscar – was awarded to Levi Strauss. Society had moved in on denim with one of its most powerful weapons – fashion.

Institutions of society, apparently threatened by an anticulture, quickly responded by identifying and weakening its effects, like antibodies detecting a virus and massing to render it harmless. From the 'creative ooze' of the anticulture emerged – the Designer! Fashion adopted, adapted and neutralized the politically provocative associations of denim. From that moment, from the first creative touch of Gloria and Calvin, the anticulture was dead, its icon – denim – appropriated by the middle, upper, and aspiring upper classes. In any case, denim had become clichéd. As the counterculture became more attractive to more people, as its ideals and icons had been sanitized for popular consumption by a more relaxed, laid-back consumer

Warhol's crotch-level view of the Stones; unzip it and see. 'Sticky Fingers' album cover, 1971.

Levi's 'Route 66' campaign.

society, most people under the age of forty possessed at least one pair of blue jeans. There were kiddie jeans, jeans for pregnant women, jeans for the family, jeans for backyard barbecues, jeans for Preppies and Sloane Rangers. As Charles James, the radical couturier remarked, blue denim was America's gift to the world. Blue jeans were as common – and as totemic – as Coca Cola.

In 1976, three or four elements combined to raise the status of denim: inflation raised the cost of clothing; bad cotton harvests caused scarcity; and a scare was raised that polyester caused skin allergies. Fourthly, denim had become banal. But people were not ready to move out of denim into other fabrics: Seventies hippies and their sympathizers were now a little older and a little (some quite a bit) richer, but they had not abandoned the ideals or the clothing conventions of their youth. They hadn't abandoned their youth, for that matter. They still stuck to denim like Linus to his security blanket. The first stage of a fashion attack is to remove a material from the price-range of the masses, and by the late 1970s denim was more expensive. The second stage is to differentiate down-home style from Fifth Avenue style, and at this point the designers moved in to experiment with denim and give it Ritzier style. Jeans took on permanent knife-edge creases, were infiltrated by Lycra, were teamed with high-status fabrics like silk and cashmere, linen and fur. Denim was worn with pearls or black tie. Jeans, which had found their spiritual home in the Klondyke and Haight-Ashbury, suddenly found themselves right at home at Harry's Bar or the Plaza.

But a funny thing happened on the way up-market. Jeans were suddenly rejected as acceptable wear in the very places they had hung out in the Sixties and Seventies – at discos, wine bars and would-be-fashionable clubs. Levi's picked up the idea and made a British television commercial about it: young dude is checked out at the door of a downtown disco club by a bouncer who lets him in because – he's wearing sharp *black* Levi's. The bouncer doesn't talk the essential fashion language. He's cool, but he's not frozen out from good times by the wrong gear. Authority is subverted by the dude's classy, ironic, private challenge to the rules. The great and the grand could wear what they liked in their usual haunts of high-style – nobody gets the bum's rush from the Ritz for wearing a pair of designer denims; but clubs, bars and restaurants for the lower, lower-middle, and middle classes were likely to bounce any patron not dressed appropriately in the high-tone casual wear sold on Main Street or in Mall mufti. Suddenly, there were no more hippies, and rockers were rejected: despite, or because, street fashion in the mid-to-late Eighties emphasized the look that the bourgeois majority hadn't yet caught up with – the Fifties. Jeans figured large in the fashion revival of the style of thirty years ago, along with slicked hair and leather jackets. James Dean lived in the image of a designer range of jeans, launched in 1987, bearing his name and portrait on the label.

Women, dyed-in-the-denim diesel dykes aside, have lived through the Women's Movement and come out – most of them – the other side. They wear jeans, as men do, less as a political statement than as comfortable pants for casual occasions. Denim was never really feminine. Fashion softened it a little, dressing it up with rhinestones, embroidery, fringing and ruffles. Fashion cut it up into skirts and jackets, puckered it, pleated it, prettified it, and perverted its essential quality of hard-wearing utilitarianism. In the Eighties, denim reverted to type – masculinity. Denim's image in the Eighties was still erotic – mainly homoerotic.

1987 brand label for Dean Jeans, licensed by the James Dean Foundation. 'Live Fast' – but don't play in traffic.

Hard-core gays in macho denim: slaves to fetish.

Advertising was aimed at men and, through men, at women. A recent British television commercial for Levi's 501s showed a young American leaving on a Greyhound bus for army duty. Taking manly leave of his girlfriend, he presses a brown paper parcel into her arms. Opening it in her bedroom, she finds it contains his favorite 501s. Sprawled on the bed, she wriggles into them and dreams of her young dude. The gift of a garment is symbolic: a lady would give her knight, her hero, a token – a handkerchief or scarf or some article of apparel as a form of sympathetic magic. In exactly the same way, the hero off to war or duty gives his jeans – the token of his power, masculinity, his virtue, his sexuality – to the woman who will have to cope without his actual presence. It's corny, but it's powerful stuff. He wears the pants – the 501s – which he gives up only in extraordinary circumstances. Denim, implicitly, is tough; denim is macho; denim is for horny boys.

Denim, to push things a little further, is gay. Gays since the late 1960s, post-Stonewall, have tended to dress aggressively. Denim is for hustlers, denim is for cruising the dangerous waterfront, denim is for the Marlboro Man and his rough-riding clones (though it's interesting to note that recent Marlboro ads have dressed the cigarette cowboy in beige pants – someone out there is getting panicky.) Denim is for crotch-watchers, for hot buns, for steamy nights on Castro for the urban lumberjack of Christopher Street. Gays assert an over-the-top masculinity as a sexual turn-on. In *Fantasia On The Seventies* Edmund White observed: "For the longest time everyone kept saying the Seventies hadn't started yet. There was no distinctive style for the decade, no flair, no slogans. The mistake we made was that we were all looking for something as startling as the Beatles, acid, Pop Art, hippies and radical politics. What actually set in was a painful and unexpected working-out of the terms the Sixties had so blithely tossed off . . . Fantasy costumes (gauze robes, beaded headache bands, mirrored vests) were replaced by the new brutalism: work boots, denim, beards and moustaches, the only concession to the old androgyny being a discreet gold earbob or ivory figa. Today nothing looks more forlorn than the faded sign in a suburban barber shop that reads 'Unisex'.'' The 'new brutalism' in Europe – and particularly in London – was typified by Punk kids who rejected denim as tainted with the sissy stuff of 'Flower Power', soft drugs, and infantile idealism. They weren't gay, particularly – they were cynical and aggressive and resentful.

They rejected denim, too, because by 1977 it had become established as designer wear for the straight middle class. In the late 1970s, Calvin Klein, Gloria Vanderbilt, and others had recognized and acted upon the need to assert conspicuous consumption and to identify a pair of jeans as a high status garment, to separate those who wished to wear jeans tastefully from those who were ignorant or scornful of the subtleties of high-fashion dress. Blue jeans worn on Rodeo Drive had to be identifiably expensive, so Calvin and Gloria stuck their names on them. Conspicuous labeling. Much was made in the fashion press of the cut, the quality, the loving attention to style detail, and the price – and more was made of the Vanderbilt name, the only really essential ingredient apart from the high price. High price, big name, high fashion, big status. In 1982, Karl Lagerfeld showed a denim suit in his collection for the Paris couture house of Chanel, and in the same year Levi Strauss sponsored a design competition at St. Martin's School of Art in London to stimulate design of classic denim fashion garments. Most of the students rejected the naff stonewash, snow wash, or any other kind of bastardized

Unisex- heterosex – denim: mean, moody, not magnificent.

ROUGH DENIM

Jo'burg Hell's Angel and mean machine.

Brighton Beach Rocker – ripped.

Trafalgar Square style – punk, rocker,

dude – tri-style denim.

denim – they went more or less exclusively for unwashed indigo denim.

They were interested in the original color and texture of pure indigo-dyed denim because they were influenced by Japanese designers like Kenzo and Miyake who had brought a native Japanese form to European and American fashion by layering, wrapping, twisting and draping rough materials such as roughly-torn, crumpled and slashed cotton, canvas, rubber and denim. This radical fashion treatment depended more on texture than on form for its effect – though form was implicit in the fabrics such as denim which imposed their own demands on the designer. The Japanese style influence resulted, in its most basic effect, in a mid-Eighties fashion – which harked back to Punk and partly derived from it – for slashing denim jeans. The 'Poor Boy' look of ripped denim jeans and jackets was Punk's last gasp, a final bid for fashion status. There are those who will, literally, rend their garments before risking any possible identification with the leisured, tasteful, rich, upper-class fashion consumers. Punk challenged social conventions and shook a fist at them through music, hair style, and physical abuse of the body. Punks who thought nothing of sticking metal through their flesh hardly blanched at tearing their clothes to shreds. The torn and tattered 'hard-times' look rejected and mocked, ironically, the glamorized hippy ethos that had firmly lodged itself up-market in style. The 'hard-times' look also parodied the original image of Rock and Roll. But soon enough ads for Calvin Klein denim showed out-at-knee jeans – and when designers begin, artistically, to rip sixty-dollar denims, to parody a parody, it's endgame. Who but the rich and/or the reckless can afford to vandalize their clothes? At this point, extremes meet: and on that dangerous edge, the middle-classes are frozen out.

Denim has become as subtle as language. Denim is – almost literally – a blank canvas: it signifies nothing in itself. The context is everything. Inflection, tone, accent, and the grammar of fashion relieves the banality of denim. A back pocket label, a waistband patch, a key ring attached to a belt loop, studs, rivets, button-fly or zip-fly, state of fading, condition of wear, inside seam, frayed or sewn leg bottoms – that's street talk, communication, credibility. Conspicuous consumption is another dialect – cut, color, a monogram – implies money, status, a refined and sophisticated knowledge of fashion subtleties. That's Fifth Avenue talk, Seventh Avenue speak. Out on the weirder fringes, Italian Fascist style, Nazi insignia, studs, zippers, snaps, transfers, deposits of grease and grime, reveal a language as finely-tuned as the engines of the motor-cycles belonging to greaser gangs and Hell's Angels. By comparison, the nerd in the suburbs in his Montgomery Ward or Sears twenty-dollar jeans is tongue-tied, sartorially speechless. Grammatically, jeans tell us that we all share a similar physical nature from the waist down. How the higher nature, from the waist up, is dressed is an indicator of social aspirations. Blue jeans bespeak sex and a sexual nature. It's just that some have more to say about it than others. Sex, not jeans, is the universal common denominator – but denim is the medium. The medium is the message: "the media do not transmit ideologies; they are themselves ideologies," remarks Umberto Eco. Denim is the universal medium, the universal ideology of the post-war world.

Exclamation marks in the grammar of fashion.

Anthony Crickmay's interpretation of what it means to wear denim: hot-riveted in the back seat.

"EMILY HAS HAD A FEW BOYFRIENDS in the past, but doesn't have one right now (get writing fellas: enclose a picture, and if you can figure out what it means to wear 501s 'but not just because they're 501s', then you're on the right track)." This was from a 1987 magazine interview with Emily Lloyd, teenage starlet of the high-grossing movie *Wish You Were Here*. Little buds and their buddies in credible Levi's 501s dig content over form: they've sat with lollipops or fingers or somebody else's tongue in their mouth in the back row of the movies and thrilled – their little gonads going and their pressure popping and their jaws working – to the 1983 Levi's commercial blistering their eyeballs with exploding orgasms of hot metal and rock faces dynamited to rubble right up there on the major screen. They've felt the thud and thump of gliding copper sheeting banged by the throbbing stamping machine and heard the rush of a million copper rivets. They've read the message – "There's rivets. And there's Levi's rivets." And they're hot-riveted to their seats as mighty forces of nature collide orgasmically, as white-hot technology is harnessed, as the hard little nipples are studded to blue denim – and all the little buds and buddies feel like towers of power in their copper-nippled Levi's blasted from hard rock and created in hot fire.

Emily's attitude to blue denim, and particularly to Levi's 501s, was professionally formed for her five years back down the yellow brick road of marketing hype in '82 by the London advertising firm of Bartle Bogle Hegarty, commissioned by Levi's to restore their flagging credibility with fifteen- to twenty-year-olds, the main target market. BBH, a new company, figured that Levi's "should be restoring the major values of toughness, durability and style". Peter Shilland, Levi's marketing services manager for northern Europe, reckoned that the mid-1980s "Levi consumer is not necessarily defined by age" – there are a lot of wrinklies out there still strutting their prime stuff in blue jeans like yesterday has still to happen – though fashion was still important to the young. "We found out that a lot of kids under twenty really did feel, and articulated quite clearly, that jeans advertising was full of clichés, which they summed up as 'all bum shots and blue skies'," said BBH, and "lifestyle advertising was seen as pretty damned patronizing . . . If you pick on one lifestyle, you turn off 95 per cent of your market . . . Lifestyle had its day. It died." Lifestyle died young – from about 1972, it had had a ten-year run.

Nineteen seventy-two was the year that blue jeans advertising stuck its labels and its money on hot ass, young butts ripe as peaches bejeaned for the be-bop lifestyle. The British brand leaders were Levi's with about 15 per cent market share, and Wranglers with 13 per cent, the rest hustling way down the averages in single figures with a product that only a no-style Neanderthal could love. If Levi's was the generic name for blue jeans, 'the real thing' like Coke, Wranglers were the blue jeans equivalent of Pepsi Cola. Blue jeans were mega-business. Levi's turnover in 1946 had been a minor-league twenty million dollars: their market had been mostly blue-collar and blue-butt cowpokes and miners who got by in forty-five different sizings of one style. Until the mid-1960s, jeans had been sold mainly on the strength of their practical function: they were tough, durable, and gave fashion the finger. In 1967, Arnie's Army Surplus Store was a better bet than Harrods or Bonwit's if you wanted a pair of jeans.

But within five years, according to Lybro jeans, "everyone from Steve McQueen and Gunter Sachs down to streetcorner yobbos wears jeans. They've become the great classless symbol –

THE TOTAL 90'S LOOK

Wrangler style for the 1990s: stonewash, raw, and broken twill denim, brass-domed rivets, and looser fit. The Urban Gipsy look.

the equivalent, in clothing terms, of the mini car. It's now the ultimate in chic to drive a mini and wear scruffy jeans." Socialite millionaires, movie stars and midnight streetcorner yobbos no longer lived lives – they had lifestyles, some sweeter than others, but nobody paid more than about fifteen bucks for the essential pair of jeans. A 'Creative Director', writing in an advertising trade magazine in 1973, commented: "Probably no single garment, outside of a religious order, has been so widely used as a synonym for a complete set of religious values, or a symbol for a change in lifestyle that is pseudo-religious in the strict sense of that much-maligned word." What he meant was that all the world, from Marin County to St. Moritz, from Haight-Ashbury to Hoboken, was hippy-casual, laid-back and wiped out, turned-on and tuned-in, free-movin', free-lovin', and free-floating. Blue jeans, tight across the hips and peachy cheeks, stretched across a generation feeling good. The 'Creative Director', the Man Who Knew Where It Was At and could roll a buck out of it, continued to decode the denim message: "What began as the hard-wearing garment of the hard-working man has been transmuted into the uniform of nonconformity – and a unisex uniform at that. It is just one example, although the most marked, of a generation's determination to turn the values of its predecessors topsy-turvy, to set its dignity at nothing and to find perverse merit in apparent trivia."

Where he was right on the rivet was when he noticed the significant appeal of blue jeans to a wider, non-committed market: "What was originally a symbol of rebellion now becomes the symbol of continuity of that movement. As long as Levi's are around, nobody's copped out." The innovator, the mouthpiece of anti-establishment values, becomes subtly assimilated into

Steve McQueen – classy classlessness on-set in lifestyle denim.

South American blues: the magical-realist camera of Sebastiao Salgado catches two captive kids in San Juan de Chimborazo, Ecuador, 1982.

ARTISTIC CREDIBILITY

Andy Warhol, artist and iconoclast, in cultivated – and thus cultic – blue jean uniform; Augustus John, artist and doyen of British bohemian apostolic in blue denim *ouvrier* mode; Ernest Hemingway and son in trout-and-stream, river-and-trees thorough *masculine* denim.

the established order of fashion and largely defused. The Class of '68 may have moved out of the streets and into the condos, abandoning their banners and some of their principles, but so long as a pair of Levi's hung in the closet, beside the college letter sweater and other battle fatigues of innocent and idealistic youth, there couldn't be much wrong – nothing that couldn't be fixed – about the good times getting better for the movers and shakers shifting their street-wise jive into the boardroom of major industry and the corridors of power.

So there were the blue denim butts of '72, bobbing and wobbling, jouncing and bouncing, bumping and be-bopping to the music of Little Richard corkscrewing into 'Good Golly Miss Molly' for Lybro jeans, not to be confused with Little Richard hot-diggety-dogging it and whooping into 'Tutti Frutti' falsetto for Levi's. The music – Fifties rock – said nothing about cowpokes or hard hats, the principal consumers of denim in that period, and everything about rebels without causes and sensual streetcorner midnight dudes. The images were reminiscent of Kenneth Anger's *Scorpio Rising*, an underground movie short, a languid classic of eroticism focusing on a motor-cycle cowboy greasing his machine and sliding sensuously into beat-up blue jeans to the sound of 'She Wore Blue Velvet'. Hip undergrounds and gays would get the reference: the grunts would get the message.

The American Dream of the 1970s, as experienced in Europe and points East, was perceived as pretty innocent and even naïve: blue jeans bespoke an apparently effortless prosperity and a self-indulgent society that could afford to be idealistic in its widespread condemnation of its own war in Vietnam and support of civil rights. In the worst of times and the best of times, jeans were expressive of youth and idealism, jeans were for hot times and good sex, jeans were

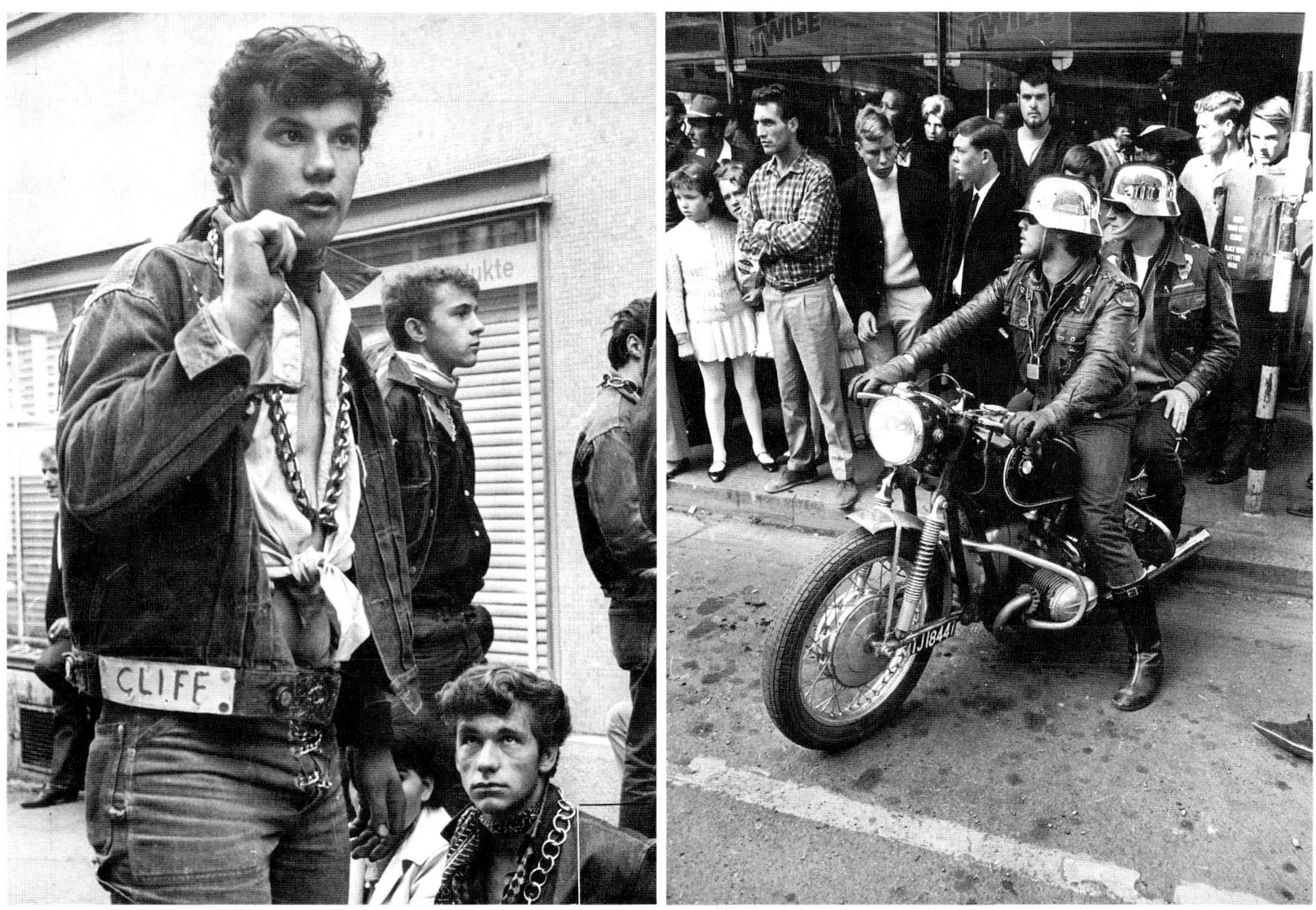

Medallion Man and Machine Men in get-down-and-get-dirty denim. Denim talks back.

Berlin communards in Euro-style denim: polymorphous perversity in the post-nuclear extended family.

Lonesome traveller sets out on the enlightenment trail in real-life denim.

for new freedoms and no fuss, for barrier breaking rather than ball-breaking.

Jeans were worn dirty and tatty, frayed and funky. Jeans were personal – customized by each and every individual body – and jeans, in the dated word of the Seventies, were more or less unisex. Women wore men's jeans, sisters and brothers under the blue denim skin. The difficulty was to sell new jeans in the Seventies, when no one would want to be caught dead (or defunked) in pressed and pristine dark indigo-colored blues. British brand leaders in '79 were Levi's with 16 per cent of the market, and Wranglers with 11 per cent, while small-time but influential fashion design retailers like the Italian Fiorucci company – purveyors of easy-sleaze and flash-trash rig to the moneyed teen-be-bop market – sold a modest eighty thousand pairs of designer jeans a year. Fiorucci jeans cost – importantly – about £25 (around $40) in Britain, compared with the normal Levi's sales tag of £15–£18 ($24–$28). About 60 per cent of jeans were sold to sixteen- to twenty-five-year-olds, according to the British company Lee Cooper, but Wrangler reckoned that their market extended up to thirty-four-year-olds reluctant to lose the last symbol of their teenage. Jeans in Europe had become widely accepted even in the most traditional areas – bank clerks in Denmark wore jeans to work.

At this point, in the late Seventies, enter Gloria Vanderbilt with all the feline poise and big cat chutzpah of a fashion jungle predator looking for a slice. Gloria had image; Gloria had a high-tone name; Gloria had Ritzy elegance; Gloria had fashion savvy. Gloria plugged a significant market gap when she acted on a fistful of hunches and parlayed them into a fashion success story for the late Seventies and early Eighties. There were at least half a dozen sub-texts to the Gloria Vanderbilt designer jean label. Underlying the logo were several nascent trends: European designers like Fiorucci had proved that price was no object for a pair of jeans hyped by razzamatazz and pzzazz. The market for jeans was wider than previously thought – from mid-teens to mid-thirties, and a significant percentage of that market was female. None of the big denim companies designed specifically for women who – surprise – were a different shape from men, and didn't want to be men; the old androgyny – unisex – was a dead decadent dream. Women were tending to look more feminine, but were reluctant to return to traditional feminine social roles and cute girly clothes. Nobody could force women back into pastel print dresses and skirts. Gloria took note that women were into pants and wouldn't be shifted out of them. Like men, they were into denim – a familiar icon of their youth – which still had a markedly male image. That image could not easily be feminized, but it could be glamorized and given an edge by hype directed at the New Woman, the Barbie Doll demanding equal terms with Action Man. With a bit of lateral thinking, not to say lateral marketing, the New Woman could be a latter-day Cinderella – out of her denim dungarees and into her Vanderbilts. Out of the kitchen and into the disco. From drudge to Vanderbilt, from Hogpatch to Sutton Place, more affluent but insecure about conspicuous consumption. Spending money was OK so long as it wasn't flagrantly ostentatious – the hippy ethos hadn't yet collapsed: the work ethic was still faintly disreputable.

But anti-fashion – hippy denim – was about to be incorporated by mainstream fashion. Ted Polhemus noted, in the mid-1970s, the upward mobility of denim at its peak: "I got invited to a party given by the Marquess of Dufferin and Ava and everybody was there: the Jaggers, David Hockney, Leonard (a London hairdresser), Peter Sellers, Liberace (the party was in his

A guy, his bike, and his woman – she in asymmetric denim skirt – on the right tracks.

WHO'S THAT GIRL?

Mean mother Fonda; Bardot balancing on a bejeaned thigh; Monroe meditating a cue in 'The Misfits'; Di showing sweet-jeaned thigh.

honor), J. Paul Getty, and a lot of titled people. Now the Marquess of Dufferin and Ava was dressed to the teeth in a very, very well broken in (if not falling apart) denim work jacket with the words 'Kansas City' inscribed on the back in metal studs. . . The point is simply that fashion is constantly devouring anti-fashion, and some pretty strange anti-fashion at that, at an alarming rate." The idea that 'dressing-up' was bourgeois and capitalistic, words that were a-hissing and a-spitting in the mouths of the hippy generation, purist in heart and appearance, did not die easily – but Gloria was the thin edge of a fashion wedge that finally did for hippie serendipity.

Design was the buzzword, and denim was the transitional object – "The 'Kansas City' jacket", says Ted Polhemus, "is, in terms of communicative significance, a different jacket when worn by the Marquess of Dufferin and Ava than it was when worn by the kind of American who originally designed and wore it. The object remained the same, but the significance of that object has been changed drastically." Denim, associated with the high-class glamour of a title and riches and power (represented by the Marquess and – equally vitally – his media mix of party guests), was ripe for reactionary revolution. Allying snob appeal with good design and the traditional idealism represented by denim was an irresistible marketing strategy. By 1982, worldwide jeans sales had jumped to a billion pairs a year. Ironically, by giving high-style to denim, Gloria and other designers moved blue jeans into the aspiring middle classes which, not classy enough to carry off a 'Kansas City' denim jacket with the flair of high rank and old money, and mildly anxious to dissociate themselves from street-level low-life denim, but not intimidated – reinforced in their glitzy dreams, rather – by designer

Delegate to Beat-Boy Convention in Zurich, 1989: a denim jacket to die for.

duds, took to the form of high-class and reassuringly expensive (though not impossibly pricey) designer denim and the hell with the content.

Designer denim was mostly for women, significantly changing the image of denim. Gloria Vanderbilt jeans were first launched on the market in 1978, in Britain in 1980. They were followed by other name brands such as Cardin, Calvin Klein, Sasson, Diane von Furstenberg, Polo Westernwear designed by Ralph Lauren for The Gap Stores, Studio 57 jeans; and eventually Levi's and other major denim companies got the message from the fashion mavens.

By 1984, sales of denim jeans and other denim garments were slipping. The hype had hiccupped. Levi Strauss announced a worldwide cutback in production. The boom year, the *annus mirabilis* of denim, had been 1981 – it took 61 per cent of the market for casual trousers, up from 46 per cent in 1979. In 1984, the percentage was an anxiety-making 59. The problem was a worrying trend towards consumer independence: "People no longer want to buy a uniform, their approach is more individualistic," reported a spokesman for Levi's, and the fitness fad had contributed to a swing towards coordinated casual wear, looser and lighter, in contrast to the corset-like grip of denim. Formal wear and casual wear became more and more indistinguishable; consumers wanted to look more elegant, more put-together, more Lycra-lithe. If a pair of Levi's jeans was likely to be immortalized as a museum piece, as an all-time terrific brand like the redundant Issigonis British Mini car, the American walkman, the Xerox copier, the Bic pen, then the answer to slipping respect in the marketplace might simply be to insist on the heritage of a great brand, to resurrect the Greatness of Levi's.

No advertising campaign or image for blue jeans has ever had the impact of the British

'Launderette' and, to a lesser degree, the associated 'Bath', commercials. In the early 1980s, after a late 1970s European slump when sales of Levi's 501s had fallen to an all-time low, sales began to revive in France even without advertising encouragement. The upswing among *Bon Chic Bon Genre* French preppies and boulevard *mecs* was a pointer to the fact that 501s had never lost cachet among discerning denim devotees. The brand was a classic, a secret signal between initiates of style. 501 was the number on the original bolt of double X denim from which the first pairs of Levi's were made in the 1860s. 501s take about 30 per cent longer to make than other jeans, and the attention to detail is precise – bar tacks with forty-two stitches to the half inch, two-rivet watch pockets, nickel fly buttons, and busted outseams. The red label, like a little flag, said it all. Nothing else like 'em. 501s were exclusive and – ironically for a product identified with classlessness – elitist among the top 15 to 20 per cent of fashion cool consumers who passed the word from mouth to mouth, and kept in touch through British magazines like *The Face, Ritz, Blitz*, and other metropolitan insider fashion fanzines.

Elitism meant that denim, in the minds of the young, was no longer associated with notions of 'freedom', as their parents saw it in the Sixties. Rediscovering Levi 501s and the posing possibilities of denim was just another chance to dress up and assume a character based in nostalgia for what they had never experienced. In the Eighties, denim was aspirational, and that, of course, was the business advertising people know best. To mass-market the classy and relatively expensive (about £30, or $48, a pair) 501 brand, Bartle Bogle Hegarty rejected the knee-jerk associations with Presley/Dean/Brando – Fifties heroes. The agency opted to stick with the quality heritage that had been successfully pushed in the 'Rivets' and 'Stitching'

Soft-shoulder – tough denim: by Valentino, 1989.

Perry Ellis presents a totemic image; poetic hair, clean jawline, lithe no-talk white T-shirt, jeans lean-cut on the hips, but loose on the legs.

commercials. "The integrity of the product demanded that we draw on the 501s' heritage, but the heritage had to be relevant to what's going on now. America, these days, is guilty until proven innocent in the eyes of the young," remarked the agency director, "and our strategy was to restore the appeal of innocence. The past can be very acceptable, but it has to be played air-conditioned."

And here's the trick: first of all, take a piece of prime beefcake finishing a workout in the slatted light filtering through the venetian blinds of his bedroom window. Hot – sweaty – time to strip off and shower. But this one's – get it – different: he steps *into* his 501s and slowly – buttons – *up.* In the bathroom – functional, tiled, no feminine cosmetics cluttering the clean room – he lies back in the bath – still wearing his 501s. He chugalugs a Coke – *from the waisted original glass bottle* and settles in for a long soak. His pumped-up biceps hug the sides of the bath. He's got all day to lie there shrinking his jeans to the soundtrack of soundalike Sam Cooke grating 'What A Wonderful World'. Shrink-to-fit Levi's were something of an anachronism in '85/'86 (the commercials were first screened the day after Christmas '85) – who could be bothered? Pre-shrunk (and, looked like, pre-worn) jeans were the dominant sellers. But the message now – in the fast-lane of the late 1980s – was, relax. Work at what's important to you. Take time – take it easy – get back to *the real thing.*

'Launderette' – or 'Laundromat', to be authentic – pulled out all the stops just short of giving us a shot of the mighty organ itself – though the fantasy was probably hotter than the real thing. 'What it means to wear 501s' was mouth-wateringly and jaw-droppingly and tongue-tinglingly stated in the person of a cute Chicano-looking model, Nick Kamen, who

Details of classic Levi Strauss 501s with essential red selvage. The real thing for style faddists.

personally stonewashes his 501s at the local laundromat. The kicker is, the kid has to drop his denims, peel off his black T-shirt, strip to his boxer shorts right there in front of the Maytag to get the job done. A ten million pounds sterling (around sixteen million dollars) European advertising campaign hung on the Kamen charisma, the Kamen pecs, the Kamen tush, to turn on the masses and still keep the loyalty of the 'Stylists' and 'Early Adopters' of 501s. While Kamen came across to the sound of Marvin Gaye's 'I Heard It Through The Grapevine', and six hundred and fifty thousand little buds and buddies rushed to climb into their 501s to express their uniqueness and individuality and their hots to have or look like Kamen, sales of rival jeans rocketed: so powerful was the media impact that Levi's, as a generic name for jeans, also helped push up a product like Lee jeans by 40 per cent without Lee having to spend a dime.

With 'Bath' and 'Launderette', Levi's reclaimed the high ground of designer jeans and re-established basic denim credibility. The new youth market of the late 1980s demanded "authentic, status-enhancing properties in the clothes it buys". The designers had tried too hard and too cleverly, so that the rising generation of denim consumers "got cynical and thought that if they were going to pay those designer prices they might as well buy real designer clothes. Jeans had become unfashionable by attempting to be too fashionable; they had lost their essential jeansiness and what the young ones want is the real thing." The same message got through to Coca Cola when they tried to introduce the new, sweeter, 'designer Coke' – the consumer wanted 'the real thing', and got it when the company called quits and restored the original flavor of the American Dream to the soft drink market.

The success of the 501s campaign knocked even the advertising agency sideways for a while.

For a time, there was a shortage of 501s to fill demand – up from 80,000 pairs a year to 650,000 – which spilled over into subsidiary successes for the background music to the commercials – the songs hit the charts again (the Sam Cooke number had first made it in 1960). Kamen kept the impressionable masses delirious, while Bartle Bogle Hegarty shrewdly moved to retain the loyalty of the cognoscenti with supporting advertisements in quality magazines, teaming 501s with status and contemporary cult classic clothes from high-style designers like Paul Smith, Scott Crolla, Joseph Ettedgui, Azzedine Alaia, and covetables like Rolex watches. The associations were soberly made, like museum exhibits, laid out flat like they'd been photographed for a Metropolitan Museum of Art or Victoria and Albert Museum catalogue. 501s, even if sold in the High Street, still had high-style.

'Bath' and 'Launderette' were profoundly layered – like all powerfully evocative creative objects – like art. The purity of the object was not compromised: 501s had remained largely unchanged since 1873. The modern image lay principally in the Fifties, described by BBH as "the classic property of youth culture". Dean, Brando, Presley, of course – but the agency consciously avoided the stereotypical associations, including the Fifties artifacts such as period cars and period music, which had been used before. The images – and the look of the heroes – were subtly updated, but underneath lay the strata of the Klondyke miner, the cowboy, the dirt and violence of the black-leather biker, the love and peace hippy, and the urban macho gay. 'Bath' and 'Launderette' had sub-texts as deep and pervasive as the underlying, unspoken tensions of a Tennessee Williams play.

The commercials were knife-edged balanced to accentuate the positive, eliminate the

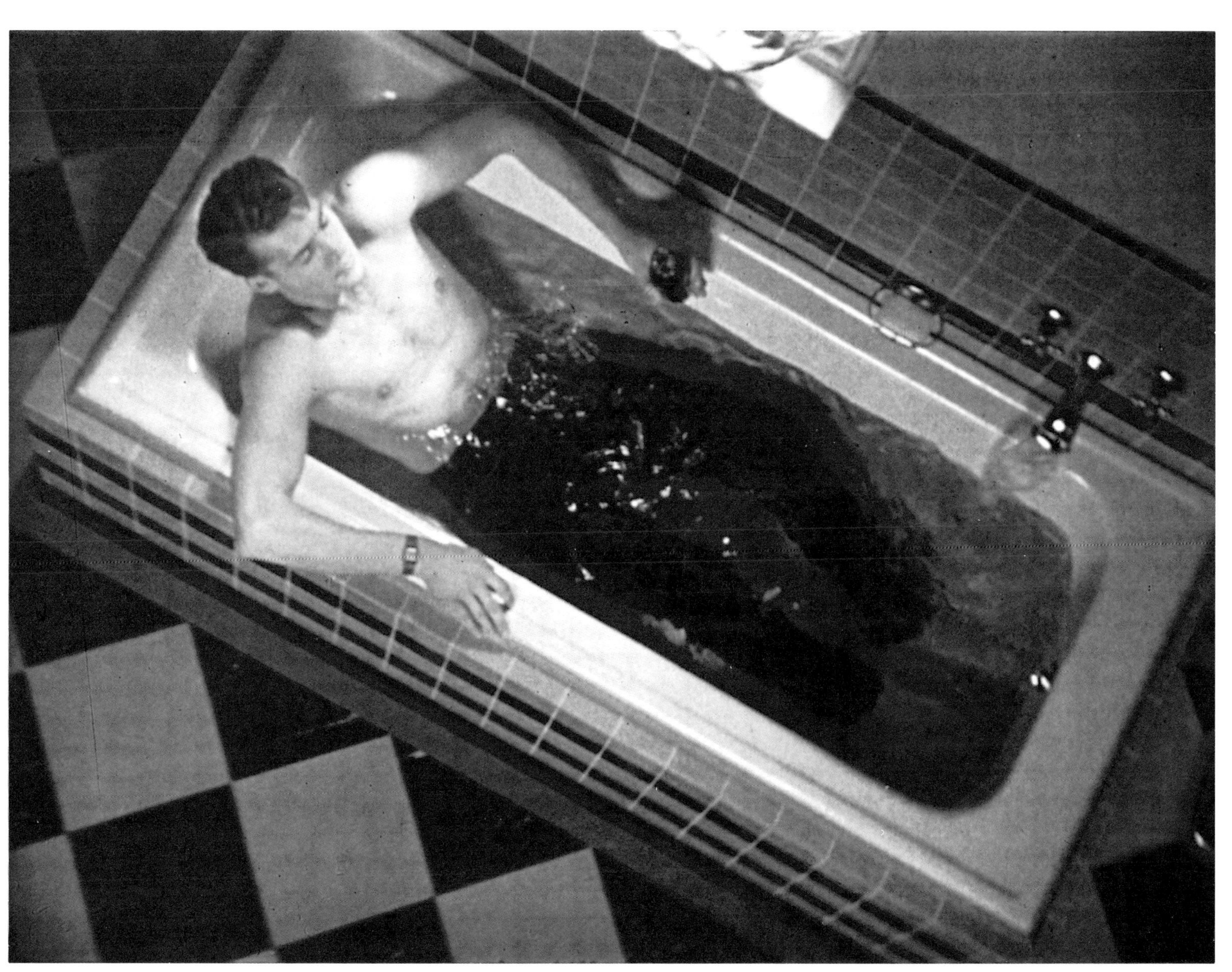

Shrink-to-fit Levi Strauss 501s: still from 'Bath' television commercial.

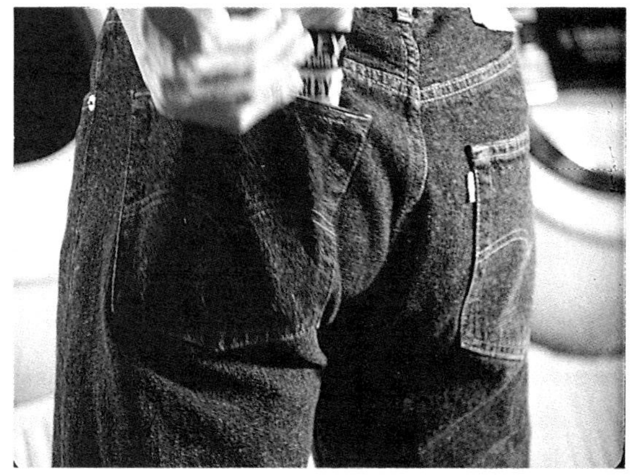

STONE WASH

Stone-wash at the laundromat – stills from 'Launderette' television commercial.

1. The ten million pound sterling tush.
2. The shot that rocketed sales of boxer shorts.
3. Kamen, getting his rocks into the Maytag.
4. So what to do? Brits only bought one pair of jeans per head.

negative associations. Tim Lindsay of BBH was reported in mid-1986 as saying: "the US is always a pretty dangerous place. As over half of all jeans are sold to the sixteen to twenty-four market, what we had to do was sell heritage without selling Ronald Reagan. The answer was to pick an almost mythical time and place that everyone in the market is familiar with, yet is sufficiently long ago for them not to know anything about." The Fifties, almost as a bonus, happened to be fashionable in the mid-1980s, and the follow-up commercials in '87 stayed put, more or less, in that ninety-second borderland of Fifties mythologies, of pony tails, Pepsi, puppy love and Presley. The Levi's promotions prompted other blue jeans brand names to pump money into advertising if only to profit from the knock-on effect of the cult 501s commercials.

The Levi's commercials were so successful in Britain that the Laundromat setting was picked up by Lee Jeans in 1988 for an American audience. The guy washing his load is puzzled by, inevitably, finding a spare sock in his wash. To a background of city street noises, an older woman/mother figure begins talking to him in absurdist vein about his "odd sock". Like some Oracle, she is full of sound advice about domestic mysteries. He should not attempt to "wash lights and dark together". Stranded in this sort of *Huis Clos* environment with this woman and a young girl, he stares wistfully at the girl's bejeaned bottom. Improbably, a title card pops up, with the words 'separate loads' and the pay-off is that the girl shyly asks the young man if he wants to borrow some soap. The atmosphere of the laundromat is evoked by a setting of venetian blinds, plastic chairs and massive industrial tumblers. He is forced to make a choice between the Mom figure and the sweet teen virgin, both offering something – experienced

VINTAGE

Dungarees from the 'American Classics' collection, and a classic Levi Strauss look – the crucial shirt and jeans.

advice on the one hand, sudsy satisfaction on the other. No contest. The British commercial for Levi's is more focused on the nonchalant narcissism of the male in a largely female environment, whereas the Lee commercial resolves the anxieties and angst of its hero in more traditional terms by allying them with the knowledge and know-how of a bejeaned little trainee *hausfrau* who will forever ensure the whiteness of his wash, find the lost sock and comfort him with the pressure of good, child-bearing hips encased in desirable denim.

With sales of designer jeans going through the roof, other jeans manufacturers began to cotton on to the value of attaching status to a brand name through advertising an image. In 1979, designer jeans had chalked up one billion dollars in sales, close to 10 per cent of the total jeans market, even though they were priced at almost three times the cost of conventional jeans. Designer jeans marketers spent about 10 per cent of annual revenues on advertising hustle compared to 2 per cent for traditional jeans. About twenty million dollars had been spent advertising status pants. Jordache Jeans, for one, successfully hyped itself within a year from low-status to high-style by spending two million dollars in 1979, 10 per cent of its twenty million dollars sales, in a determined effort to increase brand recognition and sales. The aim was to achieve a 50 per cent increase in jeans sales, up to thirty million dollars, by the end of 1979.

The company had been organized in 1978 by three Israeli brothers, Joseph, Ralph and Avi. The Jordache name came from an acronym of their names, to which they added a French-sounding 'che' for high style. Their product was manufactured in Hong Kong. Most of the money was spent on television advertising in the United States, particularly in the style-happy metropolitan area of New York. Up to thirty TV commercials a week crashed into *Good Morning America*, the evening news, the eleven o'clock news, and prime-time slots including *60 Minutes*. Prestige magazines were splattered with sexy Jordache ads – *New York Magazine, The New York Times Sunday Magazine, Playboy, Harper's Bazaar, Vogue, Time,* and *Newsweek*. Jordache Jeans were aimed at teens and twenties – kidstuff – with high styling and a callow sexuality, brooding without being boffo, cool without being cocky.

The Jordache kids were sexy but clean – High School jocks who had made a deal with Mom to press their pants and show some respect. They smoldered, sure, but they were more interested in making the team than trashing cars for kicks. Still, there was something there – something maybe unsettling about these suburbanites that could turn subversive. It was inevitable, maybe, that in the late '80s they should turn into the terrible teens, bad-mouthing bratpackers who finally turn on Mom and her attitudes. For two years, Jordache has been combing the malls and High Schools of Southern California to find kids who could whine convincingly and make faces that asked to be slapped. Two years!? It should have taken no more than two minutes. In the 1989 Jordache commercials, the Jordache Mall moppets turned into Mall monsters and uttered the line that shocked America to the roots of its Reeboks: "I hate my moth–errrr". Mom is watching TV with her tough teen blonde daughter and her Twinkie-crazed friends. "I hate that commercial," says Mom, turning off the offending Jordache plug. "That's disgusting. You're not watching this trash in my house." Authority takes a last and futile moral stand against teen liberty to go to hell in a basket. "I love that commercial," says the Mall rat and turns it back on, uttering the words, "I hate my

Rockers in nostalgic '50s mode: the look is motorhead, the message is airhead.

mother." Mom is a certifiable nut, besides looking like a middle-aged slut. The kids, by comparison, are cool and so is the commercial. This is pure late '80s stuff in image if not in popular psychology: Electra and Salome had some pretty big grievances against their mothers, too.

Jordache, points out Barbara Lippert in the March 7 '89 issue of *Adweek,* tries to have it all ways and inevitably fails. "The worst spot features these brat-packers – including a guy with massive cheek-bones and long hair, who looks like a suburban Attila the Hun – in a diner, tackling the subject of world hunger. The spot seems to cover at least four decades. The kids eat food of the '50s (chocolate pie and shakes), touch on some of the attitudes of the '60s (thinking about starving people) and imitate a movie of the '70s (*Diner*). The phony, 30-second attempt at humanity to sell blue jeans is pure '80s, however. Jordache can't, on the one hand, cash in on such subjects as mother-hating, and go for a Bob Geldof-style humanitarian prize on the other. But for consistency in delivering annoying commercials in questionable taste, Jordache gets the genius award." And, presumably, sales through teen identification with teenage confusion and hubris. Emphasis has usually been firmly on the sixteen to twenty-four-year-old age grouping. It wasn't necessary – or even desirable – to target the late twenties and thirties, because what the kids wear, the rest – turned on by images of teens and twenties – will consume out of vanity and nostalgia. They're still feelin' good in 501s or Wranglers or Calvin Kleins or Jordache, and lookin' me-too like sweet sixteen is only a matter of packaging.

Brooke Shields was a pubescent fifteen when she was hired to star in television and press

Brooke Shields bopping in her Calvin's: Eine Kleine Kiddieporn, according to some American moralists, who objected to Richard Avedon's photography.

Denim Dudes: Dean in poor-boy mode denim; Jagger in hot-lips, hot-hips denim: Lennon in sober mood denim: Springsteen rockin' in denim: Bowie belted into cool coat denim.

SH AIRWAYS
SH AIRWAYS

Designer Denim: up-market embroidered denim skirt – sleeping off a last tango in Paris.

advertisements for Calvin Klein Blue Jeans. She tucked her legs over her head and spread them wide. She wriggled and writhed, and if she didn't win the title 'Miss Jail-Bait 1980' it wasn't for the want of hype. Her career as a movie starlet had already included, at the age of nine, *Communion* in which she was stabbed to death by a religious maniac; *Pretty Baby* in which, aged eleven, she played a twelve-year-old New Orleans hooker; and *Blue Lagoon* four years later in which fifteen-year-old Shields was marooned with teen actor Christopher Atkins on a South Sea island where, without benefit of Kinsey or Spock, they finally managed to figure out the best way to satisfy their teenage libidos and – hey presto – reproduce themselves.

The Klein commercials bothered middle-America. "It's child pornography, using children in sexually enticing postures to sell a product," protested Ms. Julie Green, of Women Against Violence and Pornography in the Media. "This kind of thing can only encourage kiddie pornography." Shields had previously, blamelessly, endorsed squeaky-clean products such as Ivory Soap, Colgate toothpaste and Breck shampoo. No problem – keep the kids clean, keep America clean. Out with filth. Shields was the shining face, teeth and hair of the teen dream. Her much-vaunted virginity, her close relationship with her protective mother Teri, her virtuous refusal ever to appear nude on-screen (a stand-in had substituted for the unclothed Shields body in *Blue Lagoon*), and her perceived adolescent innocence had seduced movie audiences who found very little difficulty in separating the fictitious screen siren from the real, cute, self-respecting budlet painted to picket-fence perfection in media articles.

Calvin Klein, too, was a media superstar, though more raffish and sophisticated: his friends were the likes of Bianca Jagger, David Bowie, Andy Warhol and his Factory acolytes. He had assiduously promoted himself in association with his characteristically Euro-American-style fashions which were soft, supple, sporty and sexy. His fashion style was subtle, classic, simple: he liked "clothes that slide when the body moves". He regularly won prestigious fashion industry awards, and was saluted as a self-made fashion and media celebrity. In 1980 he launched his line of designer blue jeans, allying the status of his own name with the innocent sensuality of Brooke Shields as his model girl. Both Klein and Shields genuinely fascinated the American people who were turned on by the subtle innocence of Shields' sexuality and subtle sensuality of the apparent classic innocence of Klein's clothes. To that extent, Klein and Shields were made for one another, a match made somewhere between Hollywood and Fifth Avenue. Nobody can realistically accuse Americans of any lack of subtlety: they are more experienced than most in taking two opposed ideas and holding them in perfect tandem. This is not as easy as it sounds: it can make for severe schizophrenia unless those opposed ideas are interpreted and presented as a whole by media experts who layer them like a club sandwich.

Denim, in this case, was the transitional object between the cute, classy, nymphet-style sensuality of Shields and the celebrity status of Klein's products which, while ostensibly demure and undramatic, were associated in the public mind with Klein's high-profile social life and connections in New York. What, perhaps, middle-America objected to, and found so alarming, was the implication, in the media campaign, that Brooke Shields – America's Virgin – had consented to all the implications of Klein's hectic life-style: that she was about to be seduced into Warhol's Factory and gallery of grotesques; that she'd soon be sniffin' at Studio

Advertisements for Calvin Klein denim: good buddy jeans and jackets snapped by Bruce Weber.

54 with Steve Rubell and the big boys; that the professional child would in some disturbing manner be corrupted and tainted by the world beyond the Blue Lagoon.

The television commercials and magazine advertisements now seem perfectly inoffensive. In them, Shields swung her lithe, long legs and exposed her midriff. The pictures were taken by the most prestigious beauty and fashion photographer, Richard Avedon, who dwelt lovingly on Shields' bejeaned legs as she tossed them around with sporty facility. Calvin Klein Blue Jeans themselves were not trashy or tacky – they were demonstrably expensive, well-designed, and Klein products as a whole were regarded respectfully by most consumers. Shields, in the ads, confessed she had "seven Calvins in my closet – if they could talk, I'd be ruined". To the Moral Majority, the implication was clear – here was this sweet kid stashing away seven men in her closet, any of whom could come bounding out, ripping off his jeans, to deflower her in a minute. This sweet teen, too, had other stuff to confess: "Between me and my Calvins there's absolutely nothing." The girl didn't wear knickers. The rough kiss of denim was bestowed upon Shields' bare flesh. Her tush was touched by her Calvins. The ads were pulled by several local TV stations, in a twitch about their effect on impressionable audiences.

The campaign earned Shields anything between four hundred thousand and a million bucks – accounts of the exact amount vary from story to story in the hyped-up media. Klein's own takings from sales generated by the campaign amounted, according to some calculations, to one hundred and fifty million dollars: *The Sunday Times* of London, in September 1989, reported that sales of his blue jeans took Klein's business "from a $25 million company to a $180 million dollar company in a single year". Which was probably worth all the aggravation

Advertisements for Calvin Klein denim: big fashion, big bucks; high class, high status by Bruce Weber, the essential photographer of the 1980s.

Easy Rider in authoritative, authoritarian denim.

from Women Against Violence and Pornography in the Media: though maybe some of the hassle had its effect. In the mid-1980s, Calvin Klein turned from his previous social life and became a born-again married man extolling family virtues and the culture of clean living. His press and media campaigns, however, have not noticeably suffered from sexual inhibitions – witness the fine, clean-limbed and ass-naked models posing for ads promoting his perfumes; particularly 'Obsession'. By comparison, the Brooke Shields campaign for Calvin Klein Blue Jeans pales into sexual insignificance.

The Brooke Shields campaign for Calvin Klein Blue Jeans was wittily, sexually suggestive: but denim, rather than Shields herself – or, rather, through Shields herself – was being presented as sexy. They were, in a literal sense, blue. The choice of Avedon as photographer, like the choice of Shields as the model, was not accidental or casual – his fashion and beauty photography was a byword for high-tone hype larded with a knowing appreciation of female beauty and sexuality. Avedon was not as 'naughty' as, say, Helmut Newton – but he was wise in the ways of high fashion and celebrity photography. He knew precisely what he was doing when his lens lingered on the Shields thigh, when it travelled across the Shields tush, when it caressed the Shields crotch. It was haughty hype rather than naughty hype: there was no real intention to shatter the mass, magical illusion that Shields had preserved herself as a teen virgin. The point being made was that Shields enjoyed not only her Klein jeans but also her body and, incidentally, its effect on men whom, undeniably, she had the power to arouse. Shields as an icon of pure American womanhood, however, was perhaps more powerful than anyone reckoned. It is difficult to imagine that in Europe, beyond the sanctimonious morality

Guess What? Denim – flat-bed; street cred.

of Britain, the campaign would have caused much furor. In Europe, there is less insistence that young women remain childlike into their late teens – or, particularly, into their twenties.

If a pair of 501s counts as a classic, as a fashion statement of values beyond the ephemeral, if denim hype emphasizes tradition and a return to original values, the real thing is a matter of detail, of insider language, of attention to status signals recognizable only among an inner circle of wised up fashion fascists ('fashists') who observe a clothes code that gives no quarter to anything but authenticity. Raking through the racks of specialist vintage denim depots, they're as picky as a Duchess at Dior. A major style point of Levi's 501s was the red thread running down the inside leg seams – till 1985 when the mill that produced this vital detail closed down. Modern 501s have no red selvage, narrower leg width, smaller back pockets, and no capital E on the red tag. Vintage – going on prehistoric – 501s have extra rivets on the corners of the back pockets. Secondhand supplies of the real thing – the boilermaker 501 – are increasingly rare. Yellow-stitched Levi jackets (modern ones are stitched in orange) fetch prices that would startle Sotheby's. Fifties Levi's jackets in good condition – the styles that are two inches shorter than modern jackets, with smaller top pockets, and the jacket with distinctive pleats and bartacking, without the half-belt at the back – can fetch up to five hundred dollars. The Lee 'Stormrider' jacket with corduroy collar and 'blanket' lining is shorter, wider and more rounded on the shoulders than the Levi jacket and is preferred – at about $150 – by some connoisseurs.

Pre-worn denim is tricky for some – like using somebody else's toothbrush – and there is a difference between style sophisticates and mode-movers, though both assert status. They are

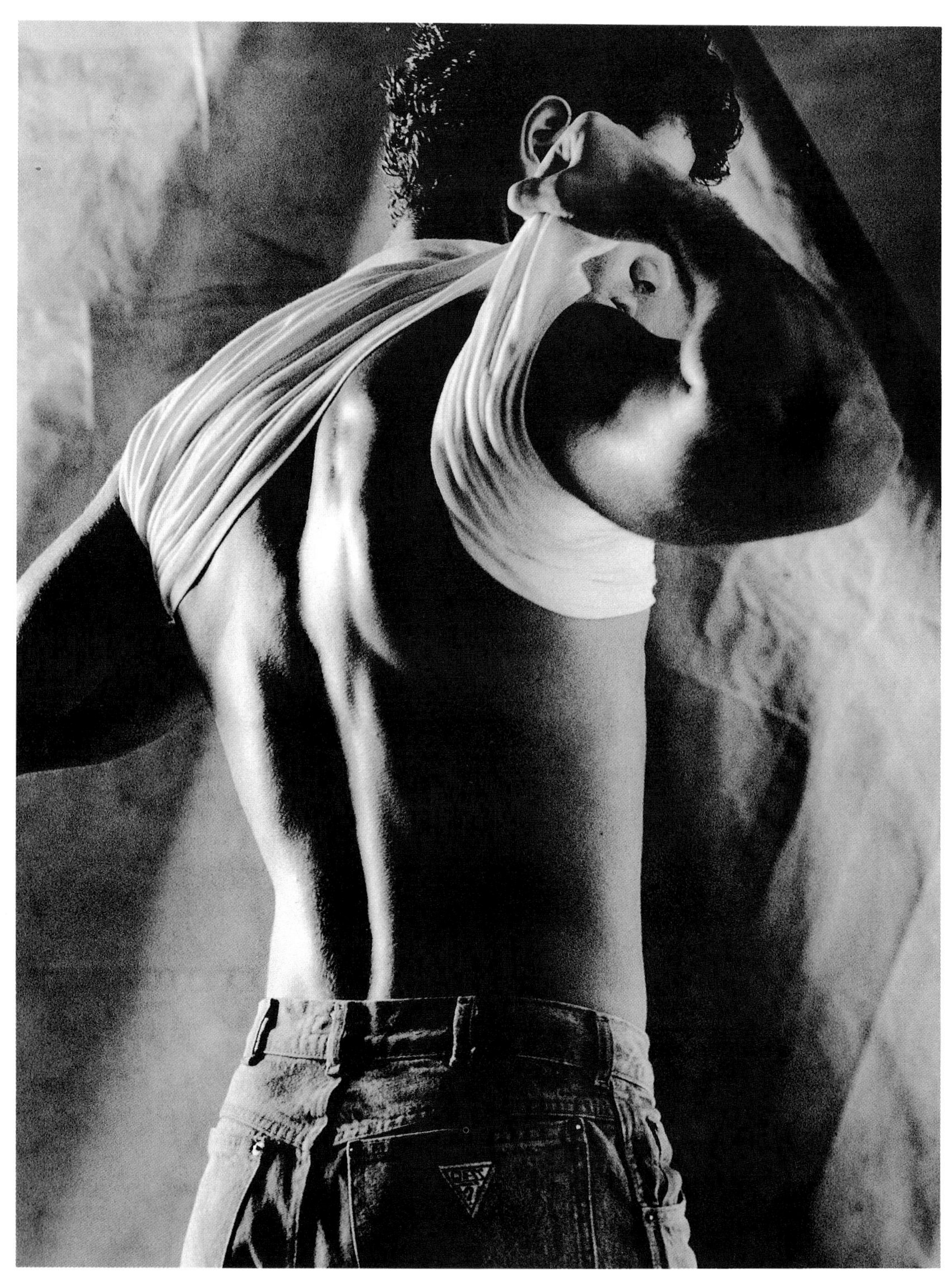

Guess Who? Classic T- and jeans. Classic torso and jeans.

both hypnotized by hype, but the stylist is a purist who, when the grunts move in on his territory, retreats into arcana to assert status. His hyper-refinement of style becomes Mandarin in its adherence to ritual detail. The modist moves on, abandoning one style for another as soon as the high ground of fashion is invaded by the hoi polloi. The trouble with denim is that *there is no alternative.* Like the black leather jacket, like chinos, like the Chesterfield coat, like the three-piece suit or the little black dress, like the navy blue blazer, like the tuxedo or the shirtwaister, blue jeans or a denim jacket count as classics. No way round that – they exist. They hang in the wardrobe, and there's not a damn thing you can do about it. So, like all classics, you can adapt them to suit the myth that fits your inner psychodrama.

Guess jeans grasped all this in '87 – they made a jeans commercial without showing the product. Guess was founded in '81 in California by the Marciano brothers – Armand, Georges, Maurice and Paul. They'd left France, in a snit about the new socialist government, and took their denim expertise in stonewash, double stonewash, bleach, double bleach, with them to L.A. where they decided to butt heads with the designer jeans market dominated in the States by Calvin Klein. Deliberately, they priced their jeans high – about seventy-five to a hundred dollars – and watched them blow out of the stores like leaves in a New England fall. First, in '85, they hired a British director, Roger Lunn, to create the mythology in a £200,000 (around $320,000) commercial titled 'Misfits', shot in the Arizona desert and evoking the Fifties, Texas, cowhands, and sexy budlets. The nostalgia for Gable and Monroe and Montgomery Clift and the wrangling West didn't hurt. The ads hit nationwide primetime TV to the tune of four million dollars, and Guess got respect. The grainy black and white commercial shifted Guess jeans to lead status among teens and twenties, and Lunn – with his partner Laura Gregory of Challenge Video – was re-hired to shoot the follow-up commercial in '87.

Lunn was right for what Paul Marciano intuitively wanted for the Guess image: "a difference, some drama, an emotional, intense moment. . . . Italian movie, Fellini atmosphere, 'Dolce Vita', 1950s St Tropez, Brigitte Bardot . . . " which he got in his black and white magazine ads photographed by Wayne Maser of *Vogue*. Like all good ads, they touched a nerve or two in popular knee-jerk morality from religious zealots and feminist hard-liners – but allegations of provoking lustful thoughts in teen America were shrugged off: Marciano committed himself "to take risks". The ads were "about sensuality and relationships between girls and guys", and if a few pieces of material got ripped, if hair got wild, if thrashing around revealed more bra and boob than was acceptable to the Moral Majority, tough shit. A twenty million dollar annual advertising budget buys a lot of clout, and anyway Guess weren't selling to hoedown Hoosiers who didn't know K-Mart from Calvin Klein. Guess annually sold about two hundred and fifty million dollars worth of jeans in prestige stores that matched the exclusive image – in Britain, in '87, the only place they could be bought was Harrods. Ninety-five per cent of sales were in the States, though advertising promoted the brand name in Britain and Europe for the five in a hundred who could afford, who would want, and not have to be told where to find, a pair of sixty quid ($96) Guess jeans. Any kid who still needed a lollipop lady to help him cross the street to the merchandise didn't know enough to wear the product.

The ultimate step taken by Marciano and Lunn was to shoot a £350,000 ($560,000)

Guess Stars. George Irving and Mandy Smith, 'The Misfits', pissed off with the paparazzi.

Mandy Smith – Tarte Tatin in a Guess denim jacket.

commercial that led the consumer subliminally, seduced by image alone, to the product. 'Paparazzi' was located in London in 1967 – the never-never land of style for the teens of the Eighties like the Fifties were for their parents. Fifteen years is a giant leap of imagination and of style for the denim image, and that new image was as much based in movie-myth as 'Misfits'. For ninety seconds actor George Irving and I-Was-A-Rolling-Stone's-Sex-Kitten celebrity sixteen-year-old (just old enough to be targeted by denim advertisers) Mandy Smith are buzzed by press photographers from the moment they step off a plane in London and hit the city streets. Irving's role is not clear even to Lunn: he could be "an arms dealer, a musician, could be a promoter". At any rate, any such type likely to wear designer stubble on a rat-sharp face; short, flat, dark hair with nowhere left to go from the temples; shades; and an aggressive style with the rat pack. Mandy Smith looks like a remix of Donna Rice and Mandy Rice-Davies. Her escort could be a politician rather than a camera-shy arms dealer – probably a Presidential candidate. Mandy's mane, honey-blonde, is tousled in the Marciano manner – it free-floats round her cheek-bones like candy floss mutating into spaghetti, and her sparkle-white teeth get a lot of exposure in her pale pink-lipped mouth that pouts and moues like she's about to balloon and pop bubblegum. She wears Sixties-going-on-Eighties miniskirts and "goes directly on the Guess image", according to Paul Marciano, who grabs that to mean – "sensual, attractive, provocative and youth".

It seems only fair that the French Marciano brothers should have re-appropriated denim – *serge de Nîmes* – after a hundred and twenty years. Blue jeans, American as apple pie for a century and more, are now *tarte* Tatin. Who'd have Guessed it?

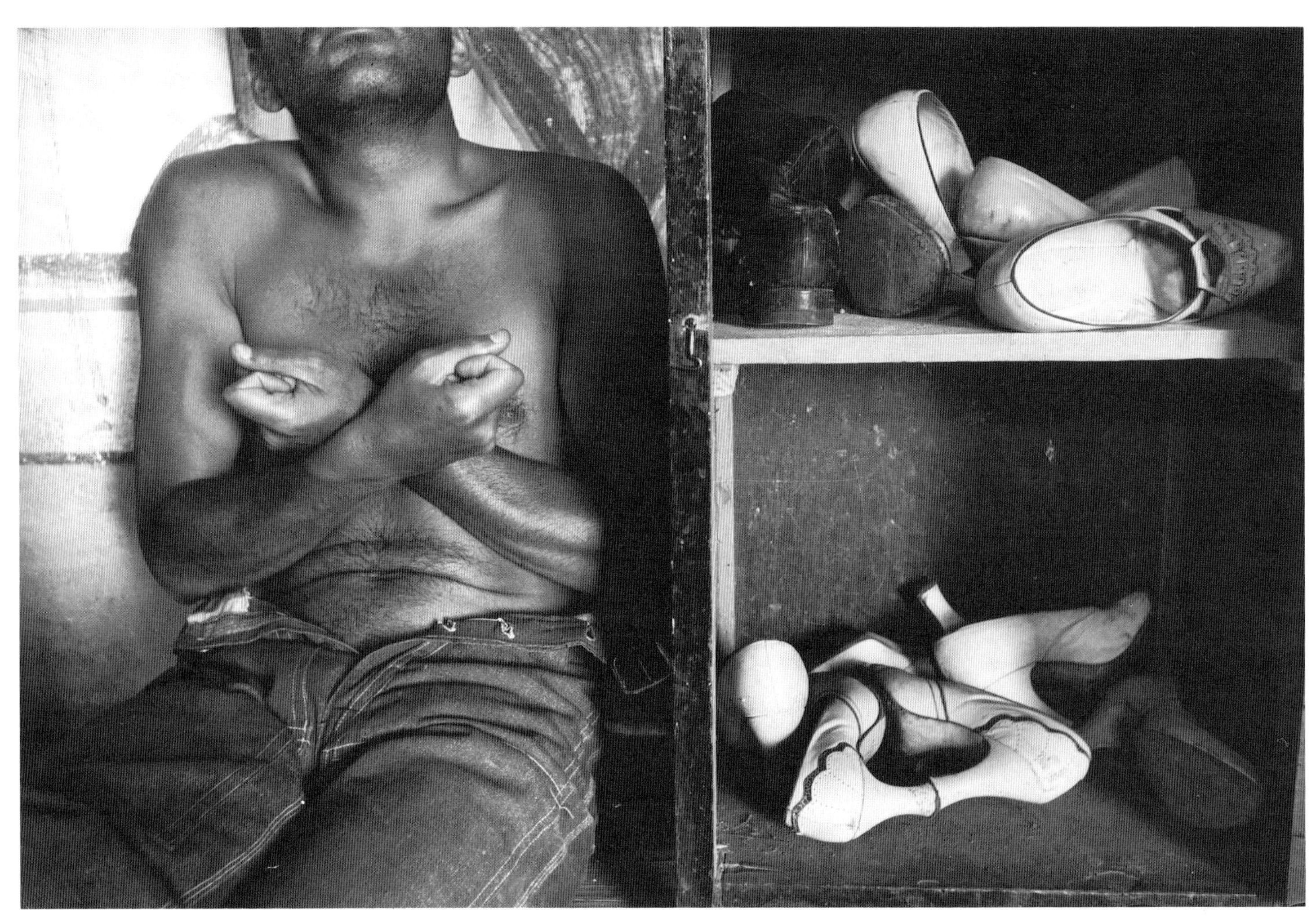

Cartier-Bresson imposes a demeanor on denim.

"A GARMENT THAT SQUEEZES THE TESTICLES makes a man think differently," observed Umberto Eco, the Italian savant of semiotics and author of *The Name of the Rose*. In particular, the adhesive effect of blue jeans against his lower body made Professor Eco "live towards the exterior world": they increased his consciousness of his body ("epidermic self-awareness") and inhibited his normal, continuous contact with his rich inner life as a philosopher. "I lived in the knowledge that I had jeans on, whereas normally we live forgetting that we're wearing undershorts or trousers. I lived for my jeans, and as a result I assumed the exterior behavior of one who wears jeans. In any case, I assumed a *demeanor.*" Women, he discovered, were already familiar with his novel experience: "all their garments are conceived to impose a demeanor – high heels, girdles, brassières, panty hose, tight sweaters." It is difficult for women to live the life of the mind when constantly preoccupied with exterior awareness. "Thought", remarked Eco, "abhors tights."

Further reflection led him to the widely-held view that tight, constricting clothing for men has always been the attire of the man of action rather than the thinker who has generally preferred looser, flowing clothes which – like a monk's habit – protect the intellectual from the distracting pressures of the world and the flesh. But the active man of the world requires a constant reminder of pressures and to be in touch with his senses, alert to deal with threats to his worldly position. Eco's thoughts turned to the Victorian bourgeois who "was stiff and formal because of stiff collars; the nineteenth-century gentleman was constrained by his tight redingotes, boots, and top hats that didn't allow brusque movements of the head." Tight jeans didn't allow Professor Eco any sudden, unconsidered movements of his legs or hips. His jeans largely dictated his posture – he no longer sprawled, slumped or threw himself energetically about the furniture, the room, or the world at large. Blue jeans rendered the normally boisterous Eco "more polite and mature".

On the face of it, Eco's response to his jeans is extraordinary – quite contrary to the association, in the popular mind and experience, of jeans with energetic leisure pursuits and relaxation. There is a paradox here: jeans are worn as much for off-duty life as working life, and they have to conform to two distinct and opposing purposes. Jeans, originally, were identified with heavy manual labor which, a hundred and fifty years later, has become glamorized by nostalgia for the age of the Klondyke and the era of the Depression when the work ethic was taken for granted as virtuous and character-building. Denim then was ample, thick, stiff, tight, and unprovocative in design, color or decoration. The psychologist J.C. Flugel considers clothing made from such a fabric to be "a symbol of the resistive strength within" – to be symbolic of the wearer's determination and grit.

Denim covered the lower (and sometimes the upper) body, and the thickness of the material protected the wearer against physical injury. The stiffness of heavy denim symbolized 'uprightness' which, by extension, implied firmness of purpose and moral probity. The tightness of denim garments, the physical pressure of thick, stiff fabric against the skin, implied firm control (like corseting) as opposed to the 'looseness' associated with frivolity and immorality. And the plain tailoring of denim jeans and jackets implied a serious attitude towards work. The good Professor Eco doesn't seem to have got much fun out of his new blue jeans – they inhibited rather than freed him. But denim nowadays has lost much of its

Cool in the tropics: denim for drop-outs.

California denim: rodeo cowboys testing a saddle, about 1930. California rodeo rider, 1920s.

◁ Oklahoma denim. Eric Hartman gets a Norman Rockwell theme.

traditional symbolism.

Denim is now a lighter-weight fabric, and its initial stiffness soon disappears after regular washing. But it still symbolizes aggressive masculinity, it is still associated with the cow-punching or gold-digging man of action, overlaid with the character of the macho biker and the inarticulate adolescent rebel who are more likely to go out and punch mouths and kick ass than sit down and quietly debate the state of the world and their place in the scheme of things. Denim is heavily overlaid with phallic symbolism. Conventionally, the stiff collar, the thick overcoat, the starched white shirt, the highly polished black shoes – the uniform of the respectable bourgeois man of business or public service – are all representative of seriousness, correctness, power, and money. They are all phallic items of clothing, associated with the power of the erect penis. They are masculine and patriarchal, symbolic of defensive and aggressive functions – like armor – and of protective and acquisitive impulses.

Denim, likewise, at the lower end of the social scale, is phallic. Denim is for the man of action, and it is generally worn tighter on the hips and legs than a normal pair of cotton or wool pants. The phallic symbolism of denim is usually exaggerated by home washing to shrink-fit a new pair of jeans, and macho men – phallic exhibitionists – will rub with a rock or wire brush at the crotch of their jeans to give the impression of heavy-duty wear in the genital region – the implication being that only constant pressure from a big, hard hump of permanently tumescent erectile tissue can do that much damage to tough material. Umberto Eco's jeans were too tight: the thinker, the introvert, will prefer looser, baggier jeans, whereas a preference for tight denim will probably signify the wearer as thoughtless, as more dogmatic,

Rodeo cowboy, 1987: sixty years on, no difference in essential style.

'Sun-glasses Ron': Mr. Cool, getting it very wrong.

more rigidly opinionated, less libertarian, less flexible in attitude towards moral principles of whatever kind. Tight jeans will project an image of defensiveness and aggression, literally of restricted ability to move freely. Looser jeans, contrarily, will signify a more *laissez-faire,* more liberated, wider-ranging attitude to life and its moral perplexities. Hippy denim was usually looser, lighter, brighter, and more imaginatively decorated than the stiff, dirty denim affected by bikers and more authoritarian groups.

A garment that squeezes the balls may make a man think differently by emphasizing sensuality over intellectualism. A guy in his tight, crotch-squeezing jeans lives in his dick – that's where the pressure is – rather than in his head. Tightness at the butt and the balls is an erotic pleasure, a kind of constant masturbation. The greaser, the hustler, and the rocker are eroticized by tight jeans. In his denim and leather, he becomes no more and no less than his phallus. With his mind blown and out to lunch, the urgent need is to get his cock blown before building up another head of pressure. Tight, resistant clothing makes us more conscious of our bodies by eroticizing the skin and the muscles which rub in constant friction against a restraining fabric and so become closely identified with it. Denim, like rubber or leather, can become fetishistic.

Black jeans, ominous in color and indicative of suppressed emotions, give no quarter. Black jeans, subversive of authority, give substance to the worst fantasies. The look is aggressively masculine, brutally elegant, a sartorial red light, an instantly identifiable urban danger signal. Black jeans conjure up bleak streets, harsh floodlighting, sinister shadows, and grim ceremonies. By comparison, blue jeans are for Boy Scouts. Brando's biker is the archetype, the heroic outsider who transcends the banal and the bourgeois. Brando is Byron in his dark aspect – mad, bad, and dangerous to know. He is Lucifer chained, confined by leather and black denim, glittering belts, buckles, zips and snaps, studs and silver metal. Getting into his uniform is like ritually putting on Samurai armor. To the adolescent urban rebel hero, the world is a dangerous place. He meets threat by becoming threatening and by covering soft vulnerability with hard defenses.

Dressed literally to kill, he becomes a walking fetish; a phallic symbol, associated not so much with the male penis as the imaginary penis of the mother – "a penis, the observed absence of which", says J.C. Flugel in *The Psychology of Clothes*, "has had much to do with the development of the 'castration complex'." One of the saddest sights is an adolescent kid, scrawny, pigeon-chested, with a little, petulant mouth and small, beady eyes half hidden under a flop of hair, lounging in the subway looking as mean as his waif-like body allows. He is wearing – a grey/blue studded denim jacket a couple of sizes too big: it drapes over his thin shoulders like someone took the hanger out of it – an ammunition belt slung across narrow hips – blue/grey jeans it would take two of him to fill – and sneakers. He could kick shit out of a passing cat, no trouble.

The man to whom denim and leather have become a fetish, the symbolic penis, is naturally reluctant to take off the symbolic clothing – to castrate himself – or to wear any other sort of garments. In 'An Interview With A Fetishist', by George Stamboulian, published in *Christopher Street*, an American magazine for gay men, the fixation is clearly explained:

"A fetish is an object, not the man himself, but so closely associated with him that it takes on

Brando – bad biker, walking fetish, Mr. Non-Congeniality.

sexual value because of that connection. Clothes, tools, and even some environments like locker rooms, ruins, and construction sites become eroticized. The classic fetishes are dick and ass coverers and extremity coverers – jockstraps, underpants, shoes, gloves. And there's protective equipment like rubber boots or a superheavy training jock that goes over your shorts when you're sparring in the ring. It's a transference of the passion for the vulnerable human skin and body to the equipment that protects that vulnerability. It's like kissing a man's armor."

Stamboulian asks: "But isn't it important for what's inside or underneath to show through – the vulnerability, the body, the sweat?" The answer is: "Absolutely. For me use and condition have so much to do with it. I like things that are salty, smoky, and have already seen some service. There's a beautiful line in *Let Us Now Praise Famous Men* where James Agee talks about Levi's and how they are a blueprint when they are brand new and how beautiful they are when they become worn and punched out." The fashion or obsession with buying used denim – the overt reason being to acquire vintage, original garments or a reluctance to buy pristine jeans – may subconsciously be a mild instance of fetishism, of repressed sexuality, of sublimated homoeroticism. And it seems likely that an obsession with worn denim and its implications or associations may be a narcissistic, self-referring auto-erotic impulse. Stamboulian's fetishist remarks: "Another problem is that gay men in those safe places we call 'Leather 'n' Levi's' bars take their cue from each other only, without ever referring back to real life. Those are the clones."

The march of the clones began in the early Seventies in New York, four or five years after

ACT-UP (Aids Coalition to Unleash Power) demo, 1989, NYC. 'CHER' is the name of an ACT-UP affinity group. Jeans represent a uniform sexuality; the T-s represent a uniform political and social aspiration.

the riot at the Stonewall Bar in June of 1969 when gay men stood up to a provocative raid on the bar by homophobic police. By '73/'74, the solidarity of the gay community was being expressed by sartorial signals quite different from the popular image of gays as effeminate fruits and fairies. "It started", wrote Peter York in the February '79 issue of *Harpers & Queen*, "with sophisticated gays who wore traditional iron-clad American men's clothes in an ironic way, as a comment that these clothes no longer had their coercive meaning. More to the point, if suburban straights were camping it up, then these clothes, these uptight blue-collar plain working man Archie Bunker get-ups, had style. There was nothing new, in principle, about gays taking up worker chic, they had been doing it for years, in eclectic little ways – a funny reference to an icon, the straight working man. But what was different this time was the way they went about it – it was so complete, such a uniform, that you might almost think these people wanted to be construction workers, footballers, lumberjacks.

"One of the tightest dress codes in the world was evolving, and with the costume – for these things can work from the outside in – a new attitude and a new/old language, the mythology of the hardman, *macho.* The costume was Basic Street Gay (or 'Lumberjack'): straight jeans, cheap plaid shirt, construction workers' yellow lace-up boots, short cropped hair – and the moustache, always the moustache." The aesthetic was fetishistic – gays identified with overt expressions of super-masculinity. They didn't only dress macho, they pumped iron and bumped up their biceps, they thickened their thighs, they whittled the waist and their shoulders shot out and their pectorals became slabs of heavy muscle. They made themselves what they most wanted to fuck, solid objects of desire. In 'Nostalgia For The Mud' by Andrew

Jeans promote subtle S&M – dirty sex: those scratch marks could be infectious.

The Christopher Street aesthetic – the gay narcissist, sexually self-aware in torn T and jeans, culturally confident, and comfortably cocksure. Photograph by Anthony Crickmay.

Holleran, published in *Christopher Street*, he reports a conversation: " 'Soon New York will be occupied by no one but the rich and the perverted,' observed my friend, and at that moment we spotted a mutual friend who embodied both these traits standing in a worn leather jacket, faded, torn blue jeans, and scuffed engineer boots, hailing a cab. 'There's a perfect example,' I said. 'Why is there that strange axis between the extremely aesthetic' – the man getting into the cab possessed an encyclopaedic knowledge of European culture and the history of ormolu – 'and the extremely sleazy?' "

These apparently conflicting aesthetic impulses – towards high culture and low sleaze – are probably connected by the super-refinement of homosexual narcissism. A taste for ormolu and for Christopher Street costume are not mutually exclusive. The clothes are 'supportive' – that is, the pleasure of wearing tight denim and heavy boots and a leather jacket derives from a displacement of skin and muscle erotism onto tight-fitting and therefore supportive clothes, and from the potency associated with them within the gay cultural code. The costume is muscular and phallic, identifying with the stimuli that animate gay society. The clothes are stereotypical, but they have been chosen with infinite care in order to give significance to the body and its sexual requirements through clothes display. The wearer is confident of his sexual identity, and chooses to fuse body and clothes into a unity that satisfies and supports his self-awareness. The display of his sexuality, through clothing conventions particular to the group with which he identifies, is uninhibited.

There's no doubt that considerable thought has been given to the outfit, and that it has been as nicely judged as by any connoisseur considering the authenticity and appropriate form of a

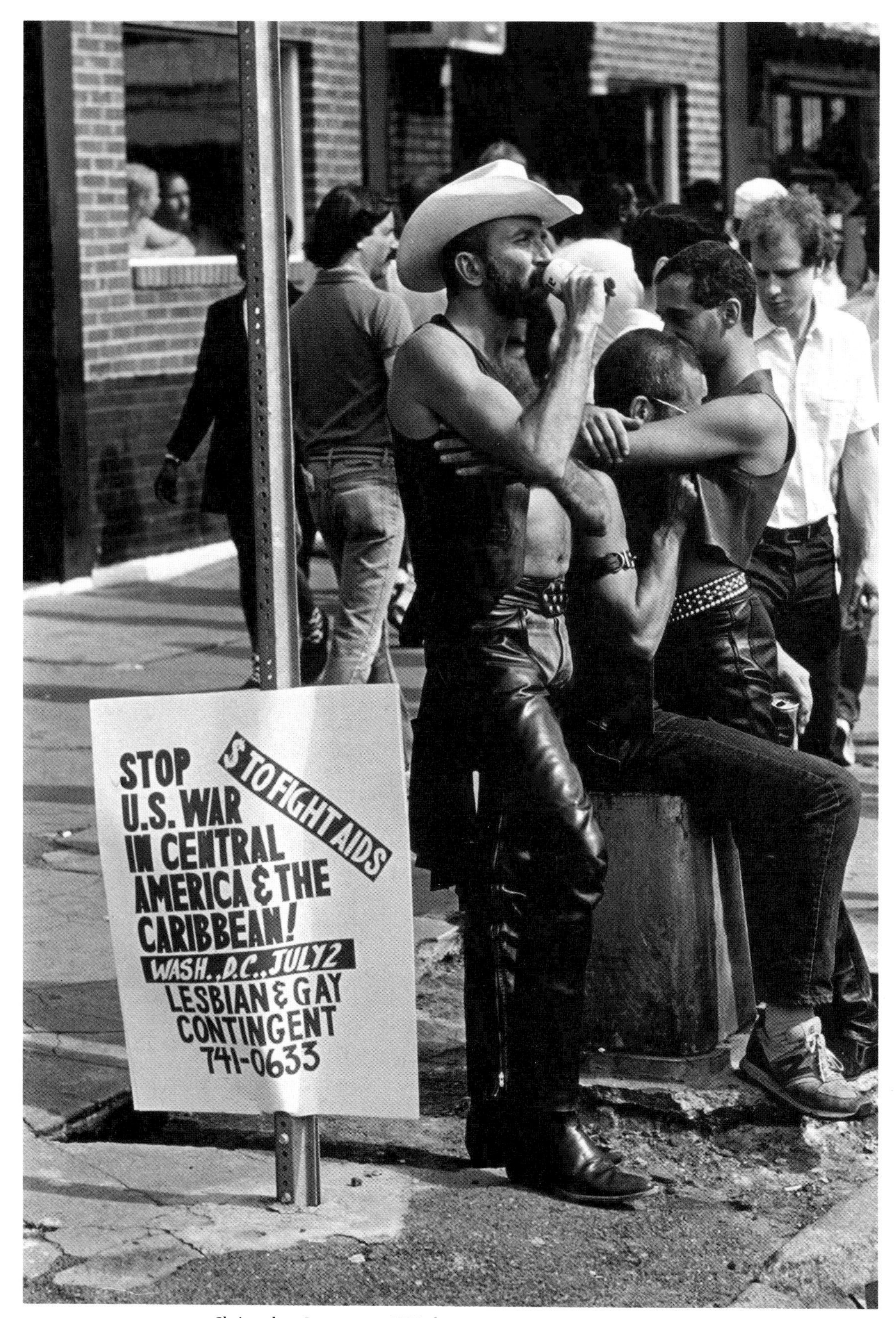

Christopher Street gays, NYC, hang out to support AIDS research spending at the expense of Pentagon spending on foreign wars.

piece of ormolu. In the narcissistic type, says J.C. Flugel, we will find the fullest capability to be satisfied by sartorial display, "and where there is present aesthetic capacity also, it is to this type that we may look for the most satisfactory development of clothes". This statement gives a substantial clue to the fact that the gay community often pioneers styles of dress that are later taken by the straight fashion world. The only disadvantage, comments Flugel, is that an excess of narcissism may lead to an excessive interest in clothes display – an interest that unduly limits the time and energy available for other things. The gay romantic narcissist was described, appropriately, through his clothes in a passage by Andrew Holleran in his 1978 novel, *Dancer From The Dance* where he describes the wardrobe of his hero, Malone, in terms that read like an extended version of F. Scott Fitzgerald's character, Daisy, in *The Great Gatsby*, marvelling over Gatsby's closet full of shirts:

"The clothes! The Ralph Lauren polo shirts, the Halston suits, the Ultrasuede jackets, T-shirts of every hue, bleached fatigues and painters' pants, plaid shirts, transparent plastic belts, denim jackets and bomber jackets, combat fatigues and old corduroys, hooded sweat shirts, baseball caps, and shoes lined up under a forest of shoe trees on the floor . . . He had scoured the army-navy surplus stores in lower Manhattan looking for T-shirts, for underwear, plaid shirts, and old, faded jeans. There was a closet hung with thirty-two plaid shirts, and a bureau filled entirely with jeans faded various shades of blue."

These, and other items, constituted a dictionary of gay-speak through the language of clothes worn by gay urban American men in the late Seventies. The outfits, in their infinite minor variations, spoke eloquently of sex: some more subtly than others. But through every

Crossbow and denim.

variation ran the common theme of denim until some, even the most sexually voracious, revolted. Holleran again, in 'Fast Food Sex', an article also published in *Christopher Street,* reported the resistance to denim as an icon of the promiscuous style of gay life. Holleran describes himself walking in Washington Square with a friend who remarks: " 'In the old days I loved the very things I loathe today – like that fellow there' (he nodded at a young man crossing the square in torn jeans, engineer boots, hooded sweatshirt, and leather jacket). 'Five years ago, the gayer the outfit the better. Someone like that struck me as a soldier of sex – devoted, in uniform, solely at the service of the only thing I lived for, sex with another man. Now' (the young man was disappearing into the trees) 'I look at him and think: how ghastly, to extinguish one's individuality, to dress as a human dildo.' "

The young man, as a foot-soldier of sex, displayed not only sexual ability, availability, and orientation, but also a powerful image of lower-class sensuality. His style of dress gave no signals indicating sexual sophistication or refinement – just the basic readiness to fuck the socks off anyone coming within five yards of his body heat. The fashion for denim and other coded garments among gays – though not exclusively among homosexual men, as the clone look penetrated the straight world where, of course, it was worn without irony – indicated a self-regarding attitude to sex, but also had meaning on another level of class distinction and sexual fantasies associated with a romantic attitude towards the working class.

In *The Language of Clothes,* Alison Lurie pointed out that a "common delusion is that members of the other classes are more highly sexed. Those who have not grown up among them often seem to believe that the rich and well-born are always at it, and feel erotic agitation at the sight of a sable coat or the label of an expensive tailor. Others think that the working class is more natural, more sensual and passionate. The latter belief has often been reflected in fashion, and is probably responsible for the popularity of carpenters' overalls, auto mechanics' jump suits and fishermen's jerseys . . . There are even people who feel that work clothes are more attractive when they are rumpled and stained, becoming the sartorial equivalent of dirty language.''

The idealism that sought innocent, frank, uncomplicated and unsophisticated sensuality in the working class, as opposed, presumably, to the complex sexual rituals and esoteric ceremonies of the lustful, corrupt, sexually experienced and blasé upper classes, was overlaid by an element of sado-masochism that derived sexual stimulation from the idea of 'rough trade' dressed in rough denim. Blue jeans, preferably the worse for wear and worn to frayed tatters in interesting places (at the tops of the thighs, either front or back, or in ribbons at the knees) promised rough and ready sex, no holds barred. In America, a popular preference was for tough young blacks, doe-eyed, brown skinned Puerto Ricans, or hunky working-class whites. The commonest sexual fantasies that regularly cropped up in pornography were sudden sexual encounters with TV repairmen, farmboys, hitch-hikers, truckers, college students, or military and sports jocks: all more likely than not to be wearing denim. Not surprisingly, faced with this hot competition, the well-to-do, well-born, and intellectual gay men tended to mimic the clothing conventions of the sexually desirable, at once identifying themselves with potent cockmanship and expressing a desire to experience it.

The phallic connotation of jeans is overt – often blatant. But the promiscuity of the late

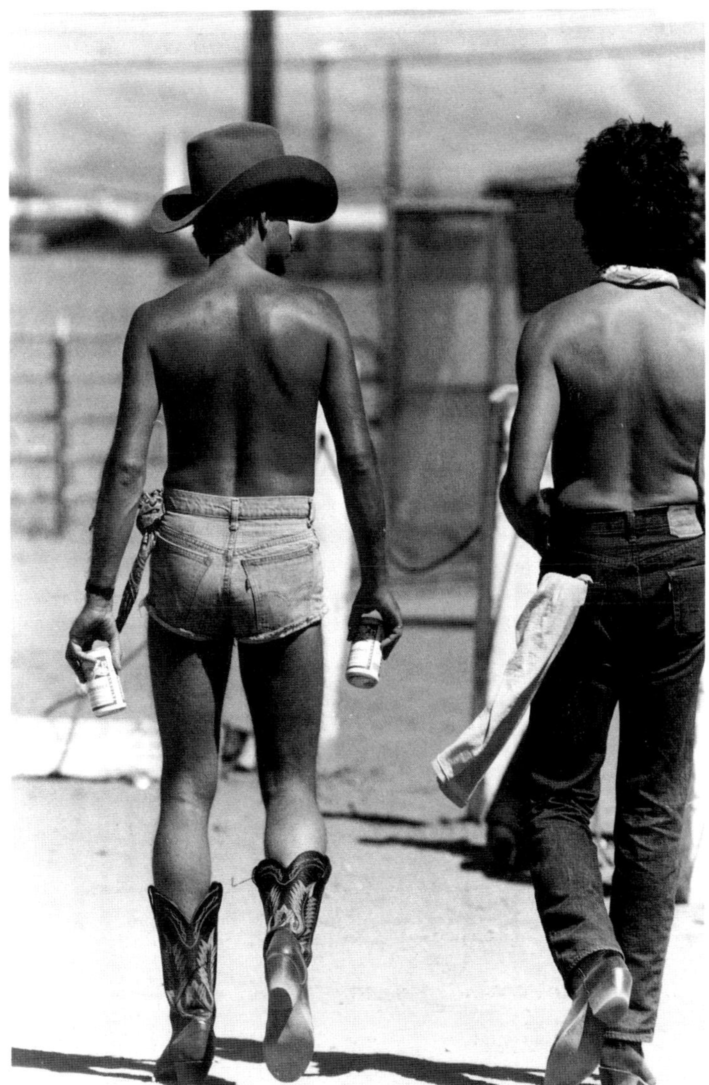

American gays, foot-soldiers in the sex war, talking dirty in denim.

A boy, his Dalmatian, and denim. Anthony Crickmay catches a tender moment.

Sixties, Seventies, and early Eighties – the period during which denim sales boomed most spectacularly – is subsiding in the generations and groups at most risk from AIDS. It is hardly surprising that men's fashion (for straight and gay men alike) has tended to return to the conventions of the successful bourgeois who asserted his potency in public and private life through his subliminally, subtly, phallic dark suit, white shirt, assertive tie, polished shoes, and expensive, stylish coat. Denim will probably lose very little of its fetishistic power to arouse homosexual men fixated on the archetypes of gay sexuality, but its potency to evoke sexual fantasy will be all the stronger for being less common. The designer jean and the cult label (such as Levi's 501) will suggest identification with an exclusive group rather than a mass phenomenon, and denim will – for the connoisseur – become a transitional object bespeaking money and insider knowledge.

Sex is, of course, inextricably linked with money – the surfeit or shortage of it. Denim is possibly more generally popular outside the United States, in the Middle and Far East, in Europe, and in Africa, to those aspiring to live the powerful American Dream, than to those trapped inside the Dream in America. The point of designer jeans was that they gave lip service to the supposed new classlessness of the Sixties and Seventies, but were perceived also as expressive of the members of a sophisticated, international social group (the designers themselves and their high-profile customers) who lived and travelled more luxuriously and conducted themselves with confidence. Confidence and security were implicit in every pair of designer jeans, and confidence was associated with more money, more prestige, more status, and better sex. The rich and the famous were supposed to be at it like rabbits. Designer jeans

Ethnic Klein

were marketed with an aspirational consumer in mind: in the August 1987 issue of *Vanity Fair*, a slick Manhattan-based magazine devoted to insider knowledge and upper-class social gossip, there were six classy advertisements for designer jeans – Calvin Klein, Perry Ellis, Ralph Lauren, George Marciano, and Esprit. There were no ads for jeans in the August 3 issue of the mass-circulation *People* magazine. This must mean something.

It may mean that the leaders of fast-lane fashion and their imitative minions, if they can be persuaded still to keep buying designer jeans, will themselves act as high-profile walking advertisements for the designers who advertise in *Vanity Fair* and hook high-class sprats to catch a shoal of pole mackerel. Blue jeans, if invested with the magic of money and style, help to bridge the gap between fantasy and reality. If movie stars, superstar musicians, TV celebrities, artists, media-hyped hustlers and society hostesses can be observed wearing exclusive, expensive designer jeans, then those jeans – which are within the price range of most ordinary people – will become associated with expensive, exclusive status and powerful sex appeal. The trick is very like that played by Paris couturiers who did not begrudge giving their most famous customers free dresses to wear at the racetrack, at parties and balls, or at other such glamorous occasions: the clothes would be admired, word would get around that such and such a designer had created them, and in theory his name – and fortune – would be made by other women mad to imitate the looks of the great and the glamorous women of the world.

The general public is a little – not much, but a little – more sophisticated nowadays. Most of us recognize that luxury objects are stage-dressing, that the posturings of the *beau monde* are

Wet, Wet, Wet in Valentino denim.

displacement activities for true power, and that real wealth and influence lie elsewhere, silent and impressive, beneath the froth and bubble of the social round avidly reported in the press by gossips. But the socialites and the liggers are up front, dressed to the teeth, collectively creating a powerful illusion of glamour and good times. By wearing denim – usually designer denim – the great and the glamorous can assert some credibility. Denim – popularly considered to be 'the real thing' – can bridge the gap between the footlights and the front stalls. By wearing denim, the rich, the famous, the well-born and the intellectual can express ironic disdain for traditional luxury and still maintain style and status by wearing designer denim or cult-label jeans which, though only one in a hundred may cotton on to the difference between Gloria Vanderbilt and Montgomery Ward mail-order, will express low-life sympathies with the masses while keeping a tightly-denimed end up with the cognoscenti.

It is surprisingly difficult to sell denim to women through sex. Denim is so much identified with masculinity that attempts to soften, to fashionalize denim merely look ludicrous and betray a lack of confidence in the essential nature and meaning of denim. Male libido is concentrated on the genital zone, and tight denim allows the male to exaggerate the potency of his penis either by the tightness of his jeans or otherwise drawing attention to the area of his crotch. Women's sexual libido is more diffuse, and they have more difficulty in displacing whole-body exhibitionism from the body to clothes. The female erogenous zone with most potency to arouse the male changes from time to time – fashion tends to emphasize different areas of a woman's body as erotically arousing, since the genital area is only one zone among many with the power to excite male libido. For a while, the back may be exposed, or the breasts emphasized, or short skirts will draw attention to the legs. Denim works best for women when fashion emphasizes the legs or the bottom as the most exciting erogenous zones, and in such cases women will prefer to wear tight jeans.

Women's fashion never, as it logically should, reveals the whole female body, and its function is to tease by combining displaced exhibitionism with actual exposure of only one or two parts of the whole body at any one time. Denim, if it cannot easily be sold to women by women as an item in their armory of sexually arousing clothes, must attract women through an appeal to the masculinity of denim. The Levi's commercial in which the young enlisted man presents his girl with his 501s is perfect. A more recent commercial shows a young girl rejecting her expensive, feminine party frock for a sweatshirt and a pair of jeans to attend a party for the rock star Eddie Cochrane. Naturally, she knocks him dead when she appears like one of the good ol'boys among the cutesy girls in their frou-frou drag. More blatantly, the trick is often to put a hunk of beefcake in close association with one female erogenous zone – a striking instance being the ad for Taverner jeans, which appeared in *The Face* magazine: a languorous toy boy lounges on one hip, with his jeans down to the tops of his thighs, one elbow on a female knee. It wasn't quite clear whether it was designed to appeal to women seeking a slave to sex or gay men goggling at the guy's exposed pubic hair. Probably both – but probably more effective in selling jeans to men than to women.

In any case, the association of denim with beefcake seems inevitable. The hunky male model has never had it so good: the tender-tough guy has a powerful appeal for women turned on by a muscled body which does not threaten violence. The Nick Kamen torso

Hot-rod denim. Anthony Crickmay says Bonjour post-coital tristesse.

successfully raised sales of 501s by several hundred per cent, and more or less naked men have helped sell anything from male toiletries to underpants through metaphorical representations of abstract power: these men are not blue-collar workers who have built up their muscles through heavy manual labor – they have pumped iron, worked out, jogged, dieted, swung weights, and crushed beer cans with their bare hands. They represent a narcissistic self-absorption that most men, gay and straight, recognize as enjoyable and desirable. This is Superstud: his time as a sex object has come. The self-absorption, the narcissism, the self-regard, is focused on "epidermic self awareness". That comforting squeeze of his 501s or his Calvin Kleins or his Guess jeans is all the reassurance he needs.